Behaviorask:
Straight Answers to
ABA Programming Questions

Bobby Newman, Ph.D., B.C.B.A.
Dana Reinecke, Ph.D., B.C.B.A.
Tammy Hammond, M.A., B.C.B.A.

ISBN # 0-9668528-5-0

Dove and Orca

This book is dedicated to John Jacobson, a friend, and a man who struggled for the right of every person to increase their personal autonomy.

Cover Design

Our thanks once again to Ken and Sharon Braun of Lounge Lizard Worldwide for our book cover conception and creation. Particular thanks go to Manny Halkas, the artist who put pen to paper to make the vision a reality. You can contact Lounge Lizard at:

Lounge Lizard Worldwide, Inc.
3500 Sunrise Highway, Suite D214
Great River, New York 11739
1-888-444-0110

For a description of their many innovative marketing and public relations services, visit www.Loungelizard.com.

Thanks also to Leo Newman, the Overlord Emeritus, for his usual tireless editing.

Table of Contents

Foreword: Should we undertake this effort?
by Bobby Newman

In an under-appreciated article from the 1970's, B. F. Skinner (1976) discussed *The Ethics of Helping People.* Reducing the discussion to its barest bones, there are three options available to us when considering people who are lacking particular skills. We can:

1.   Take care of the individuals by performing skills for them and protecting them from demands.

2.   We can attempt to ameliorate the skill deficit by teaching the skill in question to the individuals.

3.   We can attempt to circumvent the problem through adaptive technology.

To put this line of discussion into concrete terms, let us assume that an individual cannot tie his/her shoes. We have three options:

1.   We can tie the shoes for the person.

2.   We can help him/her to learn to tie the shoes.

3.   We can create some kind of technology to eliminate the need for shoe-tying (e.g., Velcro® fastening shoes).

Moving the discussion into a different area, what if a person's skill deficits were so diverse that (s)he was unable to independently function in everyday society? We would be left with two of the three previously listed options:

1.   We can provide 24 hour assistance to help the individual through troubling areas.

2.   We can help him/her to develop the skills to live independently.

Note that I do not include the third option of technological defeat of the deficits. This is merely a pragmatic alteration. We are now talking about such a global group of delays that it is not practical at our current stage of knowledge to use adaptive technology to eliminate the deficits in a single effort. Such a medical operation, for example, is still largely the realm of speculative fiction (e.g., *Flowers for Algernon*). Perhaps one day this will become an option, and medical intervention will become available. To cite one historical example, this was indeed the case when cochlear implant technology advanced sufficiently to address certain types of auditory disabilities.

A new ethical problem arose with the advent of cochlear implant technology. What if the individual under consideration does not want our assistance? Within the deaf subculture, there are some individuals who consider deafness as part of their identity and not as a disability. They would not voluntarily undergo the operations that might restore their hearing. A similar discussion has begun among some individuals advocating for individuals diagnosed with autistic-spectrum disorders (including some self-advocates).

This is an extremely emotion-laden area, both for parents who are seeking treatment for their children, as well as for individuals who are diagnosed with autism and are advocating on behalf of themselves or others. Consider the following quote from Jim Sinclair: "Therefore, when parents say, I wish my child did not have autism, what they're really saying is, I wish the autistic child I have did not exist, and I had a different (non-autistic) child instead." (Quote from Jim Sinclair's "Don't Mourn for Us" which appeared in the Autism Network International newsletter, Our Voice, 1(3), 1993. http://web.syr.edu/%7Ejisincla/dontmourn.htm)

Such statements cannot help but provoke emotional responses, and it has made it hard for each side to listen to the other. To demonstrate my own bias, not accepting that the individual cannot speak, slams his head into the floor, or relates in a different way is not the same as not loving or supporting the individual. Such parents are trying to teach their offspring (children or adults) skills that will allow them the greatest degree of autonomy possible. I think this is a goal we can all agree is a good one.

The autistic-spectrum disorders are a group of neurologically-based syndromes that generally lead to a restricted range of behaviors, as well as difficulties with socialization and communication skills. There is an enormous functioning range within the autistic spectrum. It no more makes sense to talk about a nonspecific "person diagnosed with autism" than it makes sense to speak of a nonspecific "religious person." If I told you that someone was religious, but gave you no additional information, what would you know about the person? What would you know of their worship practices, their dietary habits, or their holiday celebrations? Naturally, you would know nothing. Suppose now that I told you that a person was "autistic." What do you know? Can the person speak? How fluently and how abstractly can (s)he speak? Does the person have the ability to socially initiate to others, or to accept initiations? Is the person unduly affected by stimuli that people within the population at large generally ignore? Does the person exhibit excessive ritualistic or perseverative behavior?

The functional skills of people diagnosed with autism range from some individuals who may be able to function independently within society (at least in some areas) right through individuals who will not learn to communicate, follow simple requests, tolerate the proximity of others without self-injury, or even to toilet independently without intensive help. The discussion of whether or not to attempt to ameliorate the behavioral excesses and deficits associated with autistic-spectrum disorders requires an appreciation of this simple fact. Without intensive intervention, many individuals diagnosed with autism will not learn the skills that will allow them to live independent lives. Please note that this is not denied by self-advocates. For example, Sinclair posits, "Your autistic child may learn to talk, may attend regular classes in school, may go to college, drive a car, live independently, have a career. . . . Or your autistic child may never speak, may graduate from a self-contained special education classroom to a sheltered activity program or a residential facility, may need lifelong full-time care and supervision."

In framing this discussion, Sinclair speaks on behalf of people diagnosed with autism and notes that "the ways we relate are *different.*" This brings us to a crucial issue. Is autism a disorder, or is it a variation of the human condition? If you consider it a disorder, of course you would recommend treatment. If you did not consider autism to be a disorder, you might think that you would advocate against providing treatment, and some have indeed taken this extreme position. But note the following from Sinclair:

> The role of professionals should be to help people use their natural processes to learn and grow. . . . It might mean teaching self-monitoring and self-management of behavior and emotions. Probably it always means learning and teaching translation skills to enable people with different communication systems to communicate with each other. . . There is no inherent conflict between accepting and working with autism on one hand, and promoting increased skill development on the other. . . . I take the view instead that autistic people, like all people, need to be taught to behave in such a way that they do not intrude on other people's boundaries. If a student is displaying behavior that actively interferes with other people... then it is appropriate to intervene, regardless of whether the student is autistic or not.
> Jim Sinclair, *Is Cure a Goal?*
> http://web.syr.edu/~jisincla/cure.htm

I believe that this is where we can find our area of agreement, and this leads to a rejection of the extremist "do not treat" argument. Treatment is teaching. We can all agree that teaching must be done, and it is then a matter of deciding what we will work on and how. Everyone agrees that increasing the autonomy of individuals, increasing their ability to make choices for their own lives, is a key goal. I would therefore argue that we have an ethical responsibility to provide treatment/teaching.

The basic argument comes down to this: if I don't have a skill, I don't have a choice. Once I have been taught how to interact with others and how to function in mainstream environments, then I have a choice as to whether to do so or not. If I have never learned these skills, however, then I have no choice. I will wind up with a lifetime of supervised care. To withhold intervention that might allow the person to avoid this condition, all the while assuring the individual that we are doing this in his/her own best interests, "respecting dignity and individuality," strikes me as a bit hollow. Suppose you were the individual who, without treatment, was destined to be standing alone in a corner of an institution, dependent on everyone around you to take care of even your most basic needs, rocking your body perseveratively and eliminating in your clothing, unable to sample even the most basic enjoyment that life has to offer. Would you like someone who could speak and could interact in the everyday world speaking on your behalf and counseling against treatment? While I admit that I am speaking as a non-autistic person in making this statement, I wouldn't consider that to be in my best interest.

If you've made the decision that you agree with this assessment and wish to undertake behavioral programming for someone you care about, this book is for you. This book is meant to be a compilation of some of the most common questions facing those undertaking behavioral programming. An effort has been made to provide explanations of any technical terms that are used, but the book was written with those who have at least something of a background in the basics of ABA in mind. While of course there are "how to" elements, the book is intended to further that background and will allow for more considered decision-making rather than function as a step-by-step guide. If I may be allowed a bit of shameless self-promotion, the book *Behaviorspeak* (co-authored by myself, Ken Reeve, Sharon Reeve and Carolyn Ryan) will provide a background for the vocabulary used in this book. Some of the resources listed in our reference section provide more of the step-by-step "how to" guide for specific programming issues.

Chapter I
Opening Issues to Consider

1. How important is diagnosis?

Generally speaking, diagnosis is not as crucial as the specific behavioral deficits and excesses identified as problematic for the learner. In other words, a student may be diagnosed with Autism, Pervasive Developmental Disorder, Trisomy 21, Mental Retardation, or Mixed Expressive and Receptive Language Delays. None of that tells us specifically, however, what the individual can and cannot do. In order to design effective programming, careful assessments of acquired and currently demonstrated skills versus lagging skills are more important than any specific diagnosis.

That being said, however, certain diagnoses do have physiological aspects that may be relevant for programming. When this is the case, a diagnosis can help us design treatments to address physiological difficulties that contribute to behavioral deficits and excesses. To the extent this is the case, diagnosis may be relevant. Many students diagnosed with autistic-spectrum disorders demonstrate excessive ritualistic behavior, for example. If one is armed with this knowledge, one may investigate variables one might otherwise have missed (e.g., Charlop & Greenberg, 1985).

When discussing the autistic-spectrum disorders (ASDs), we are dealing with a diagnosis that allows for an enormous functioning range. As stated in the foreword, to hear that a person is autistic tells you little of use. The person may have a very different behavioral repertoire, and a very different underlying neurology, than another person who carries the same diagnosis.

2. What does a diagnosis of autism or ASD mean?

We recommend conceptualizing autism or ASD simply as a series of behavioral excesses and deficits. In other words, the person is doing many things that others of his age are not doing (excesses). Conversely, he is not doing many things that his typically-developing peers are doing (deficits). Programming is meant to teach the skills that are lagging (deficits) and to eliminate the inappropriate behavior (excesses). We often encourage parents and staff to think of the student diagnosed with autism as a typically-developing person with a number of specific behavioral excesses and deficits. When these excesses and deficits are eliminated, you will be left with a person like any other who is unremarkable except for his history.

This encouragement, of course, is not meant to minimize any disabilities, nor the stress or implications that may be associated with them. Nor is it meant to be insulting to individuals diagnosed with autistic-spectrum disorders, just as it is not meant to be insulting to people who are deaf to refer them as "non-hearing" or to seek out possible ways to enhance hearing in those who cannot. This suggestion simply provides a means of conceptualizing what may otherwise be overwhelming for some people to grasp.

The best available evidence suggests that autism is a neurobiological disorder, even if the specific cause or causes remain elusive. In many cases, we are unable to know what is actually "going on inside" (neurologically speaking). We must be careful not to jump to conclusions regarding what we think is happening.

Consider, for example, as common an issue as failure to make eye contact. Parents and staff will sometimes ask "why doesn't she *want* to make eye contact?" Note that the belief implicit in the question is that the student is willfully avoiding eye contact for some idiosyncratic reason. Perhaps, however, there is another answer. Perhaps the student *wants* to make eye contact, but she tends to be so distracted by ambient stimuli that she is unable to focus sufficiently to make eye contact. Is it possible that the student "wants" to make eye contact following a request, but a bit of dust floating in her peripheral vision involuntarily draws her gaze? Reports of sensory distractibility from some individuals with ASDs support this conclusion, in at least some cases (Bailey, Hatton, Mesibov, Ament and Skinner, 2000).

The moral of our story is that a student may not voluntarily be acting is some aberrant way. The aberrant behavior may be the result of a skill deficit (inability to screen out ambient stimuli) as opposed to something voluntary. When designing treatment, objective descriptions of behavior are more valuable than causal assumptions.

3. Why choose Applied Behavior Analysis (ABA)?

There is an easy answer to this one. Applied Behavior Analysis (ABA) is the only intervention that has received empirical support as an effective treatment for autism. The Clinical Practice Guideline for Autism and PDD published by the New York State Department of Health (1999) distinguishes ABA from other possible treatment modalities as the only method of intervention that is strongly recommended in the treatment of young children with autism (U.S. Surgeon General's Report on Mental Health - Autism Section, 1999, http://www.surgeongeneral.gov/library/ mentalhealth/chapter3/sec6.html#autism).

ABA is a self-correcting system, wherein the data that are collected guide the decision-making process. The collection and analysis of information regarding progress is constant, resulting in minimal periods of ineffective treatment or lack of behavioral and educational progress. This is quite in contrast to other systems, where ineffective treatments may be provided for months or even years, without any indication that the treatment is useless. A basic philosophy of ABA is that the student is always right – that is, the environment must be altered and used to support appropriate behavior. ABA is effective by definition (Baer, Wolf, & Risley, 1968); that means that if behavior is not being changed for the better, ABA is not being done properly. We cannot simply wait for students to magically "get it." We have to provide an intensive instructional scheme wherein progress is constantly measured, treatment plans changed in keeping with that data, and where a substantial literature of empirically-validated treatments exists to guide future programming.

4. What are the elements of Applied Behavior Analytic thinking?

As outlined in Appendix One of *Graduated Applied Behavior Analysis* (Newman, Reinecke, Birch & Blausten, 2002), ABA rests on several philosophical and procedural pillars. These pillars are:

A. Procedures are based upon the principles of learning and the experimental analysis of behavior, and the research literature that surrounds these parallel areas.

B. An emphasis on behavioral determinism. Behavior does not just occur randomly. Behavior is lawful and predictable. When we understand the science and the variables in effect, we can predict and control behavior.

C. Data-based decision making: programmatic decisions are based upon the objective data collected, and not upon individual opinion or preferences of the interventionists.

D. Single-subject designs: each individual is a study unto him/herself. We can never assume that a student will respond to given interventions in precisely the same way as previous students. They must all be viewed as individuals.

E. Socially significant behavior, referring to skills and behavior that will measurably improve the student's life, are the targets of intervention.

F. An emphasis on reinforcing appropriate behavior, rather than punishing inappropriate behavior ("catch 'em being good!").

G. Observable behavior is the subject matter, not vague descriptions of what we think may be going on inside the person.

H. An emphasis on the analysis of variables controlling behavior here and now, not historical influences on behavior.

I. Criteria for behavior goals are stated very precisely.

J. All behavior management techniques are known and available to everyone (including the student). For generalization and consistency, everyone in the person's life must be familiar with the techniques being used. Nothing is secret.

5. What model within ABA? (Discrete Trial Teaching/ Verbal Behavior/Positive Behavioral Support, etc.)

That is the one question that you are *not* allowed to ask. Regardless of the specific collection of procedures, the name of the person selling the package, or the academic allegiance of the practitioner, all real ABA is based in the same science and should be comparable and interchangeable. Discussions of the model in place are distractions from the real goal of teaching and from other appropriate questions. The only worthwhile discussions to have are:

A. What teaching and behavior management techniques are being used with this learner?

B. What does the clinical literature tell us regarding the effective use of this particular technique?

C. What data are we collecting to evaluate the effectiveness of this technique?

D. What does the data analysis tell us regarding the effectiveness of this technique for this learner?

E. If the technique proves ineffective, what other techniques can we pull from the empirical literature?

Discussion of everything else is a distracting detail or a personality conflict, both of which are unnecessary and quite annoying (not to mention generally bad manners). When discussions center on the particular model being used, it is simply a distraction from the real issues listed above. The only accomplishments of talking about models are, 1) we can become a "club member" for a particular model, and 2) we can make enemies with members of the other clubs. As much as we all love a good team jacket, it is best to redirect discussions to the above issues and to avoid falling into the trap of talking about these so-called models.

As a final note on this, it is important to maintain a very clear distinction between science and political philosophy. A science of behavior tells you how to answer questions regarding human behavior, such as the most efficient means of teaching a skill. Political philosophy is concerned with greater societal issues and is not currently practiced as an empirical science. It is our very strong belief that the science and the politics must be kept separate, or at least explicitly defined as separate in discussion.

Many individuals within the Positive Behavioral Support literature, for example, seem to be attempting to wed the science to a political philosophy. For an example of this, see Jackson and

8

Panyan (2002) regarding the topic of inclusion. Statements are made about societal progress, based upon a philosophy of education and "social justice" (e.g., pp. 72-75). Regardless of whether or not you find the argument compelling, this is quite simply outside the area of a data-based discussion regarding whether what is being offered by the inclusion setting delivers the intensity of instruction required by the learner in question, or if (s)he has yet developed the skills to progress meaningfully within the setting. Those who are interested in understanding Positive Behavioral Support are also referred to Carr and Sidener (2002), as well as a powerful symposium at the 2004 Association for Behavior Analysis conference, with papers written by Drs. Richard Foxx, James Mulick and John Jacobson (symposium entitled "The Empire Strikes Back").

6. Why do professionals disagree on some fundamental issues (e.g., how much discrete trial versus natural environmental teaching)?

The short answer to this question is that programmers are also behaving organisms. Their behavior is shaped as surely as is the behavior of every other person (and living animal) in the Universe. Their professional behavior will have been shaped by their own experiences, including their initial training and subsequent clinical experiences.

Let's look at training first. Some individuals have studied at programs where professors emphasized discrete trial teaching. We can further break this down, with some people having had trainers who emphasized errorless learning methods, while others had trainers who emphasized no-no prompting (or some other system). Some individuals were simply never exposed to other models, and thus have not had the opportunity to experience their effects first-hand. While it is important for professionals to learn about all the various models in existence (e.g., via conferences and professional education), early training unquestionably creates biases that guide future practice.

Now let's look at clinical experiences. Personal experiences here also play a strong role. At my clinical office, for example, I (BN) often see students who have been involved in toilet training that is not going particularly well. *That is why they are being brought to see me,* to see if I can figure out how to jumpstart progress. In other words, there is a strong *selection bias* in effect. I see many students who are not acquiring toileting skills easily, *but I don't see the multitudes of students who are acquiring toileting skills easily. They simply aren't brought to my office, as they are already doing well.* If I didn't have a school program where I saw hundreds of students doing quite well with standard toilet training methods, I might erroneously conclude that the standard procedures are not very effective.

Dr. James Partington, during a very interesting talk at the 2004 conference of the New York State Association for Behavior Analysis made the same point as regards discrete trial teaching. Some professionals, particularly in geographic areas where poorly trained agencies provide a great deal of discrete trial teaching via a "cookie cutter" system, see a great many students who are not learning easily. That does not mean that discrete trial teaching is not effective, but it can appear that way if student after student appears at your office not doing well with the system. It may be that the instruction is being offered poorly. Or it may be that these individual students who are coming to your office are simply not showing progress, even if the discrete trial teaching is being provided well. Because it is such a powerful and often misunderstood technique, we have included a section on discrete trial teaching in Chapter XV rather than try to introduce the topic in detail here in the opening section.

As stated above, our solution to this "which model" question is quite simple. We forbid people to talk to us about particular models. We insist that they only tell us which teaching methods they are using, and show us the data that demonstrate how effective or ineffective they are. We can then talk about altering or not altering that particular technique(s), without getting bogged down in extra "model" baggage.

As a final note on the matter, be sure to read original sources. As Yogi Berra once stated, "I never said a lot of those things I said." In other words, primary sources are not always reported accurately in secondary sources. The Sundberg and Partington (1998) text entitled *Teaching Language to Children with Autism or other Developmental Disabilities,* for example, is widely cited on internet web-pages in support of a natural environmental teaching (NET) approach to the exclusion of discrete trial teaching. While the NET approach is described in great detail, a combination of NET and discrete trial teaching is actually advocated in the text.

7. What two words should precede nearly every answer in Applied Behavior Analysis?

Those two words are "it depends." Of course, you have to know *what* "it depends" on, but you generally can't go wrong by beginning this way. To explain why this is the case, we must steal (or at least respectfully borrow) a favorite line from Dr. Raymond Romanczyk: "this *IS* Rocket Science."

In all seriousness, providing an answer to nearly any question within Applied Behavior Analysis requires information regarding a myriad of factors. To take one simple but dramatic example, how should one respond to Self-injurious Behavior (S.I.B.)? Of course, *it depends*. Depending on the function of the behavior, different behavior management strategies are appropriate. Let us assume that S.I.B. is being demonstrated for avoidance reasons (to terminate an interaction, let's say). In this case, we would not withdraw the demand when S.I.B. occurs, to avoid reinforcing and thus maintaining the behavior. On the other hand, S.I.B. could be found to occur for attention-seeking reasons. In this case, it would be appropriate to avoid interacting with the student when S.I.B. occurs. Although the behavior is the same in form, different strategies would be effective in reducing it depending on the function.

The same logic could be applied to any programmatic question. Should we teach an augmentative communication system? Should we hold out for a perfectly pronounced verbal response? Should we begin mainstreaming activities? The answers to each of these questions depend on a multitude of individual factors, each of which will have to be considered in order to provide an appropriate answer.

We have always found this to be one of the toughest aspects of providing seminars in behavior management. Often, participants have specific questions regarding behavior being displayed by their children or students. We're sure "we need to do a functional analysis to answer that" is not the answer that was expected or desired. We can explore as many factors as possible during the course of the seminar, but it is unlikely we can come to a solid answer. The relevant data will need to be gathered in the setting where the behavior is occurring before we can move ahead effectively and responsibly.

Chapter II

Planning for an ABA Program

8. What are the components of programming?

Applied behavior analytic programming generally consists of three simultaneous efforts, *which are on-going throughout the life of the program*:

    A.   The teaching of new skills.

    B.   Managing of behavior that is interfering (competing) with the learning process.

    C.   Generalizing skills that have been developed into new situations and less restrictive (more "normal") environments, and the maintenance of these skills.

Any good program should have all three elements being addressed. Failure to include any of the three will impact the functional usefulness of the program. Each of these areas are further addressed throughout this book (see Chapters III, X, and XI for a start).

9. What skills should we work on?

The answer to this question refers back to our previous discussion of the importance of considering the specific behavioral deficits and excesses that are problematic for the individual. It is important to carefully assess acquired and currently demonstrated skills versus lagging skills (i.e., conduct a baseline; see Chapter IX, Question #45 and #46). For the skills that are lagging, we should set priorities for which of those skills to target first. Any behavioral excesses that prevent the learner from participating in an instructional setting or that are interfering with the teaching process should similarly be prioritized. We must also consider ways to teach new skills by building upon previously acquired skills. For example, have imitation or instruction-following or visual discrimination abilities been developed? Teaching prerequisite skills such as imitation, instruction-following and visual discrimination may be required before moving on to more complex skills.

It is often helpful to utilize a comprehensive curriculum to guide goal selections. One such example is the Individualized Goal Selection (I.G.S.) curriculum (Romanczyk, Lockshin, & Matey, 1982/1996). Regardless of the curriculum chosen, however, there are two main considerations when selecting goals:

1. Will the attainment of this goal help the learner to live a more independent life by building functional skills?

2. Are there any pre-requisite skills that will be necessary to develop prior to teaching this skill?

Remember that no pre-set curriculum is appropriate for all learners. A learner with several close-aged siblings may require a turn-taking program before an only child who has not yet begun mainstreaming, for example. A child whose parent has a visual disability may require a program teaching her to respond to the instruction "come here" as an overriding priority. Such specific considerations aside, the basics of being able to communicate wants and needs appropriately, interact appropriately with others verbally and nonverbally, discriminate stimuli in the environment and identify/categorize/properly use them, imitate others, follow directions, play appropriately alone and with others, and engage in self-help skills are more universal.

The Individualized Goal Selection (I.G.S.) Curriculum makes use of an acronym, "G.R.I.P."). These letters stand for Growth, Relationships, Independence, and Participation. Keeping this acronym in mind may help with selecting a full range of goals to target behavioral excesses, skill deficits, interactions with others, daily living skills, and involvement in the community.

10. How do I know what a "competing behavior" is?

The great temptation here is to say that it is difficult to come up with a description of what it is, but you know it when you see it. Basically stated, competing behavior is any behavior that is interfering with the individual acquiring new skills, or is interfering with the student being able to successfully function within a given setting. Some questions and examples to guide your thinking on this one: does the individual engage in resistant behavior when someone attempts to teach him (e.g., tantrums, aggression, self-injurious behavior)? Can he wait on line or take turns? Can he sit through a movie or eat a meal in a restaurant without making sounds that are disturbing to other patrons? Any behavior that is interfering with the individual learning new skills or preventing his successful involvement in the activities of everyday life should probably be targeted for intervention.

11. How do we target a skill?

The key to targeting a skill is specifying exactly what you are attempting to teach (e.g., Lovaas, 2003). As we will hammer home repeatedly, a basic rule is to "assume nothing." The fact that the person can touch his nose when you demonstrate the movement and say "do this" does *not* assure that the person will be able to perform the same movement when you say "touch your nose" or vice versa. Both the direction-following and the gross motor imitation movements will need to be acquired, and the presence of one will have little bearing on the presence of the other. To take the example a step farther, the fact that a student can identify emotions in a picture has no bearing on his/her ability to identify when another person is angry or sad in real life, or to express when personally angry or sad or happy (or whatever).

Let's assume that you are attempting to teach someone to mand (a mand is a request under a motivating condition). As Skinner (1957) himself pointed out, the fact that you teach a person to utter the label for the item when doing verbal imitation (an echoic) does *not* mean that the person will be able to use that word to actually make a request. If you want the utterance to be functionally used as a request or a mand, then you should practice the skill in a manding context. The student uttering the word "ball," for example, would lead to the delivery of a ball. Ultimately, the student would say the word "ball" without a prior model or any antecedent other than motivation for the ball (see Chapter XI, Question 57 for more about teaching manding skills).

Remember as a general rule to take advantage of "teachable moments." We mentioned the "labeling of emotions" program previously. We mentioned that the person's ability to label a picture may have no bearing on his/her ability to label his/her own emotional state. To teach this, you may have to wait for the actual emotion to be present (for real or contrived reasons) and to teach it at that moment. Unfortunately, the best time to teach "ow" and "hurt" or "sad" may be when the student has accidentally fallen down. The same would go for happier emotions.

12. What is a behavior treatment plan?

A behavior treatment plan is a written description of environmental manipulations designed to increase or decrease behavior. A major component is often how individuals in the student's environment should respond if a given target behavior occurs, or if a given target behavior does not occur. The plan should specify the following:

A. A precise description of what behavior is targeted for increase or decrease (to ensure no confusion as to when to implement).

B. How the specific procedures are referred to in the clinical literature (for gathering relevant information from the literature).

C. How to carry out the plan in practical terms.

D. The rationale for choosing this particular technique versus other available techniques (see Chapter XVI, Questions #94, #95 and #96 on functional assessment).

E. Any considerations or special information interventionists need to know that are particular to this individual (to ensure safe implementation of plan).

F. The data collection system (to gather information to guide adjustments of the plan).

G. When one should stop doing the plan (see Chapter XIV, Question #79 on mastery criterion).

As will be described below, a behavior treatment plan is *not* synonymous with "how to react." There are times when a behavior treatment plan calls for no reaction, and often a behavior treatment plan calls for how to reinforce when the behavior is *not* occurring.

13. Should we incorporate other treatment models outside ABA?

The short answer is to stick with what has been proven to be effective. To clearly address this issue, we must invoke an analysis provided by psychologist Arnold A. Lazarus (1989). Please hang with us for a few paragraphs while we explain how this is the case.

Dr. Lazarus drew a distinction between "technical eclecticism" and "theoretical eclecticism." Technical eclecticism refers to choosing individual techniques from the clinical literature. Theoretical eclecticism refers to moving around within the myriad of ideas regarding what causes a particular disorder and how it should be treated.

Dr. Lazarus suggests that we can successfully engage in technical eclecticism, but should avoid theoretical eclecticism. In other words, if a particular *technique* can be empirically demonstrated to be effective, that technique can effectively be employed while leaving behind any untested or untestable theoretical baggage, or other techniques that have not been verified as effective.

Let us take the example of "sensory" treatments. Treatments based on sensory integrative theory feature a variety of sensory experiences for the student (e.g., deep physical pressure or brushing). These treatments have not been empirically verified as effective in the clinical literature (e.g., Ingersoll & Goldstein, 1993; Lovaas, 2003). So can any of the treatment techniques be used in any way? Let us take a clinical example (Newman, 2004).

A family sought a consultation with me (BN) due to aggressive behavior being displayed by a young girl in the family. Not to put it indelicately, the girl was pulling out her mother's hair in large clumps. Gathering background regarding the behavior, it was revealed that a school-based staff member had recommended sensory experiences such as brushing and massage when the girl was being aggressive. I had seen a nearly exact instance some three years earlier with another student (see "Oh, you want to be a pizza" in *Graduated Applied Behavior Analysis* (Newman, Reinecke, Birch & Blausten, 2002)). I therefore had an inkling what was going on and recommended a reversal of contingencies. Rather than provide the sensory experiences when aggression was displayed, the sensory experiences would be provided on a schedule, *as long as that the girl had not displayed any aggression within the preceding time period.* By reversing the contingency, aggression did not lead to the reinforcing sensory experiences, but rather delayed their onset significantly. Aggression reduced dramatically within the first day, and was at zero levels within a couple of days.

Did using sensory experiences within my treatment make me a bad behavior analyst? I would certainly hope not. I expressed skepticism to the family that the sensory experiences were in any way necessary, but if the family was determined to use the sensory techniques, the techniques should at least be used in a way consistent with behavioral theory. The data demonstrated quite dramatically that the sensory experiences were indeed reinforcers and could be used within the modified Differential Reinforcement of Other behavior (D.R.O.) plan we put into place. As with other D.R.O. plans, the intervals until sensory pressure were gradually increased and therefore used less and less often, with an eye towards their eventual elimination. Suppose that a *carefully designed* experiment *demonstrated* that a student attended and achieved at a higher level following being pushed on a swing for one minute than if the session did not begin with this brief experience. Would I be a good behavior analyst if I ignored this fact? No, that would make me an awful behavior analyst (and probably very unpleasant to deal with). I can incorporate a given technique into a well-designed behavior treatment plan, as long as I maintain my dedication to data-based decision-making.

Dr. Lazarus called his technically eclectic approach "Multimodal" therapy. He warned us, however, that we cannot always combine techniques that are derived from different theories.

He called this attempt to combine different theories "Multimuddle" therapy. Anyone seeking to combine techniques from different approaches must be very wary of the degree to which different approaches can be combined. Different theories hold different viewpoints regarding treatment goals and methods, and these are not always compatible. I nearly caused an international incident once while speaking on a panel in Greece when another presenter (not a behavior analyst) suggested that recovery from autism is a myth and that the person with autism would "always be autistic in his heart," regardless of skills acquired. This person suggested that attempting to teach a person with autism to stop engaging in ritualistic behavior was a mistake. Rather, the rituals should be encouraged in the form of rote work tasks. Five minutes earlier, I had suggested how and why we might attempt to eliminate such ritualistic behavior. How could our approaches be combined? I don't believe they could be effectively combined. To attempt to do so would lead to an Orwellian oxymoron. Attempting to combine different approaches often leads you into treatment impasses. The only solution is to maintain one's dedication to data-based decision-making and to only apply techniques that can be empirically verified as effective.

Chapter III

Essential Concepts for Team Members

14. What is shaping?

Shaping is a powerful and basic process used to create new behavior. This is done by differentially reinforcing successive approximations to a target behavior.

Shaping procedures are often supplemented by prompting procedures when teaching new skills to a learner. The general steps of the basic shaping procedure are as follows:

A. Determine the best approximation of the target behavior that the student can perform. Begin by reinforcing that approximation of the response.

B. When this response becomes stable, put that crude approximation on extinction, meaning that you do not reinforce the approximation again.

C. When the behavior is put on extinction, an extinction burst will generally be seen (see below). As a part of the extinction burst, there will generally be some variability in the behavior.

D. As a result of this behavioral variability, a closer approximation to the target behavior may be emitted.

E. Reinforce this closer approximation.

F. Repeat the process from A-E until the target response is emitted perfectly.

Note: Pure shaping does not consist of the use of prompts. When teaching new skills, however, prompts are often used in conjunction with shaping. Using prompts to help the learner produce the required response helps to speed skill acquisition and reduce possible frustration for the learner when a previously accepted response is no longer reinforced. Prompts may include verbal, gestural, physical and visual cues. (See question 56 for more information on prompting strategies).

15. What is chaining?

Chaining is the name given to a set of teaching procedures that link together the various individual steps that make up a longer, more complex behavior. Referring back to the previous section on shaping, could you effectively shape a behavior such as tying shoes? It would be difficult, due to the numerous steps involved. Instead, one would first construct a task analysis of each of the individual steps (see next question). One would then shape the individual steps and link them together in the chain. This can be done by working from the first step through the last (forward chaining), from the last step to the first step (backward chaining), or through presenting the entire task at once (total task presentation). When doing a chaining procedure, remember to work not just on the most current step, but on each step the student has mastered up to that point on the task analysis. Remember, this is a chain. The individual steps are meaningless unless they are in the context of having performed the prior steps.

16. What is a task analysis?

As alluded to above, a task analysis is a written list of all the steps that comprise a complex, multi-step behavior. It cannot be over-emphasized that task analyses must be written with the skill level of the individual in mind. Depending on pre-existing skills, a task analysis for a skill like riding a bicycle might include ten steps, or might include several dozen steps. We generally recommend that you begin teaching with a given generic task analysis. When the student begins to plateau, meaning to be stuck on a given step, that step probably needs to be broken down further. It is rare to begin teaching a skill with a generic task analysis and to be entirely successful with that same task analysis. The same task analysis will rarely effectively teach a skill to two different individuals of very different skill levels. The key, as always, is to let the data guide the decision-making process. Rewrite the task analysis as needed throughout the teaching process to keep progress continuing.

17. What is generalization?

Generalization refers to the tendency of the individual to emit the same behavior under differing conditions (stimulus generalization) and/or to emit variations on the same behavior (response generalization). An example of stimulus generalization would be when a student can return a greeting to an unfamiliar person, while response generalization would be seen when the student says "hi" instead of the "hello" that (s)he has been practicing.

The importance of generalization cannot be over-emphasized. Unfortunately, the performance of many students with autism is characterized by "failure to generalize." The student does not spontaneously perform the same behavior when conditions change, or continues to engage in the same old behavior without variation. An early classic (Stokes & Baer, 1977) noted that we must plan and program for generalization – we cannot expect it to occur spontaneously. As the saying goes in ABA, "assume nothing." A student may be able to perform a particular skill in a particular way in response to a given stimulus. Don't assume that this same skill can be performed under varying circumstances. See Chapter XIV, Question #78 for a discussion of how to encourage generalization.

18. What is maintenance?

This topic is every bit as important as generalization, and often every bit as ignored. Maintenance refers to the continued performance of a behavior by an individual following the termination of the formal treatment plan. To program for maintenance, one must plan for ways to ensure that the behavior change continues to be supported following the removal of the formal treatment plan. Some formal and relatively easy ways to program for maintenance do exist.

One simple way to program for maintenance is to place the target behavior on progressively leaner and leaner schedules of intermittent reinforcement. Intermittent reinforcement tends to lead to behavior that is more resistant to extinction (continues when reinforcement is no longer occurring). (See Chapter XIII, Question #69 for further discussion on intermittent reinforcement.)

Another strategy is to teach self-management skills to the individual. If the person becomes able to monitor and provide consequences for his/her own behavior, (s)he will be able to maintain the behavior in the absence of an outside interventionist.

The most straight-forward strategy to ensure maintenance is to ensure that the treatment plan never actually ends, until it can be faded to the natural contingencies of everyday life. Training others in the setting, or the setting to which the individual is headed, to continue the treatment plan will lead to maintenance of the skill (provided the procedures are carried out correctly).

19. What are "receptive" and "expressive" skills?

Receptive tasks are those that call for the student to follow a direction given by an interventionist. For example, the student might place a block on top of a dresser after he has heard the request "put the block on top of the dresser." An expressive task calls for the student to give information to another person. For example, following the placement of the block, the student might be asked to tell where the block is currently located. Please note that while many people equate expressive skills with speaking, this need not be the case. Many students will participate in expressive tasks via some form of augmentative communication (e.g., sign language, picture exchange, or written communication). See Chapter X, Question #53 for cautions regarding working on receptive and expressive drills together.

Chapter IV

Designing an ABA Program

20. How many hours of programming?

In one sense, this is a meaningless question. As remarked in a previous work, ABA is not a related service (Newman, 1999). Intervention is on-going, 24 hours a day. That is not to say that parents, teachers, and students are involved in active programming 24/7, but they are always involved in maintaining treatment plans and working towards generalization of skills at all times.

The Clinical Practice Guideline for Autism and PDD published by the New York State Department of Health Early Intervention Program (1999) recommends that intensive behavioral programs include a minimum of 20 hours per week of direct instruction. The guidelines caution that the exact number of hours needed for each child will vary, depending on a number of variables (i.e., age, progress of the child, severity of autism, tolerance of the child for the intervention, and family participation). The guidelines also recommend monitoring the progress of the child and reviewing the number of direct intervention hours provided to determine if the number of hours needs to be increased or decreased.

Unfortunately, the recommendation for a minimum of 20 hours of programming per week suggests that at the end of the last formal session of the day, all the work is done. For skills to be maintained and generalized across settings, the strategies used during intensive programming often need to be extended outside the teaching session. Many families come to view ABA as a "way of life." These families successfully incorporate principles of reinforcement and aspects of their child's programming into the family's daily routines.

Dr. James Mulick summed this issue up beautifully at a recent conference of the New York State Association for Behavior Analysis (2004). He cited the various research study outcomes. He then asked a fundamental question regarding how much time the individual in question is engaging in inappropriate "autistic-like" behavior. It is imperative to fill up all that time so that the person does not continue to practice those behaviors.

It is important to note that professionals make varying recommendations, often suggesting more intensive intervention than the guidelines suggest. According to Green (1995):

> For young children with autism, the treatment of choice is intensive application of the methods of applied behavior analysis. "Intensive" means one-to-one treatment in which carefully planned learning opportunities are provided and reinforced at a high rate by trained therapists and teachers for *at least 30 (preferably 40) hours a week, 7 days a week, for at least two years.* Young autistic children who received less intensive treatment made some modest gains, but normal or near-normal functioning was achieved reliably only when treatment was provided for 30 - 40 hours a week, on average, for at least two years (e.g.

Anderson, et al, 1987; Birnbrauer & Leach, 1993; Fenske, et al, 1987; Lovaas, 1987; Maurice, 1993; McEachin, Smith & Lovaas, 1993; Perry, Cohen & DeCarlo, 1995; Smith, 1993).

(Quote and references taken from the web page of the Association for Science in Autism Treatment, http://www.asatonline.org/about_autism/autism_info 06.html)

Leaf and McEachin (1999) examine the literature and reach a similar conclusion.

21. Should parents conduct intensive teaching sessions?

As with many other issues within Applied Behavior Analytic programming, there are different schools of thought on this issue.

On the one hand, some people suggest that parents are meant to be just that, parents. They are responsible for the generalization and maintenance of skills, but should not be involved in the intensive teaching portion of programmatic time, either to keep boundaries clear or to protect against "burn out."

Answering back are some who suggest that intensive behavioral intervention is useless unless parents conduct actual sessions themselves. Such individuals reason that generalization will be at its highest, and parental carryover of programs at its best, if the parents are intimately aware of all procedures through being trained to carry them out in the intensive teaching environment. Also, if parents are able to fully carry out intensive teaching sessions, they will be able to substitute in the all too common event of staff cancellation. This is also a morale booster for hired staff, as they see the parents working for the behavioral gains, and know that this is not a situation of "fix it for me."

We tend to pull towards the side of having parents conduct actual sessions, if at all possible. Sometimes this will not be possible, but the potential gains can outweigh the potential downsides. See also a discussion of this topic in Leaf and McEachin (1999). Regardless of where you fall in this discussion, it is crucial that parents carry through on programmatic goals outside of "intensive" teaching time. It is pointless to work on "yes and no" drills while sitting in teaching chairs, for example, and then to have breakfast presented to the student without a single question regarding his or her wants being posed. The practice in the chairs is one thing. If the skill is not practiced to completion in the real-world setting, however, we may as well have not done the intensive teaching in the first place.

22. Is ABA only appropriate for small children?

Absolutely not. This is one of the unfortunate enduring myths about Applied Behavior Analysis. The truth is that the science of behavior can be applied to any behavior of any individual. There is no reference made here to age or diagnosis (or lack thereof). To be blunt about it, the principles of ABA can be used to teach someone to play golf just as appropriately as they can be to help someone learn to speak or to reduce a competing behavior such as self-injury.

Dr. Mecca Chiesa (2004) demonstrated this point beautifully in a paper that bore the intriguing title, "ABA is not a therapy for autism." Wait a minute! ABA isn't a therapy for autism? So what the heck is this book about? Don't miss the point. ABA is *not just* a therapy for autism. Yes, it can be expertly applied to address difficulties associated with autism, but that is not the *only* application of the science. As stated above, it can be applied towards teaching skills and managing behaviors across ages, diagnoses (or lack thereof), behavior areas, or, for that matter, even species. Most of all, for the purposes of this book, we want to emphasize that the science of ABA can help *all* people with ASD, at all ages and levels of need for intervention. No one is too old, young, high- or low-functioning for ABA.

Chapter V

Data Collection

23. What sort of data should we collect?

To address this question, let me report a conversation I (BN) once had at a cocktail party that was a fund-raiser for a particular charitable organization (while I'm in no way opposed to cocktails, such gatherings are not generally my favorite type of event). My own lack of social skills aside, a woman at the party casually commented to me that at her school, they didn't allow a particular type of behaviorally-based data to be collected. I expressed mild shock, trying not to live up to my reputation of a trouble-maker. To willingly ignore a whole body of clinical literature and empirically-verified data collection techniques made no sense to me.

A central component of applied behavior analysis is data-based decision-making. What types of data should be collected in clinical situations? Collect whatever data are necessary to make clinical decisions, end of story. Depending on the situation, that might mean rate, fluency, percent correct, trial by trial, probe data, latency, duration, magnitude, or a number of others. Don't get needlessly hemmed in. See Cooper, Heron and Heward (1987) for a wide variety of data collection strategies and when/why you might use each.

Accurate, meaningful data are necessary to effectively analyze behavior. Sherlock Holmes refused to compose a theory until all the facts were in. You need the facts to build a theory, not the other way around. If you don't follow this simple advice, facts wind up being twisted to meet theories, rather than the more correct practice of theories being twisted to meet facts.

24. Should we take data on both skill acquisition and the presence of competing behavior?

Yes. Remember what brought ABA to the dance. ABA means *demonstrably effective* teaching and behavior management. The appropriate collection of data is the only way to ensure that your techniques are doing the intended job, and not wasting the student's time or perhaps even accidentally worsening behavior.

Data must be collected regarding all aspects of the treatment program. If we are attempting to teach a new skill, how do we know that anything is actually being learned if we are not taking data on skill performance? Likewise, if we are putting a behavior management procedure in place to reduce the frequency of a given behavior, how do we know if it is working properly unless we collect data to track the frequency of the behavior? We must always take data to ensure that our teaching techniques are properly imparting the skill or that behavior plans are producing the desired effect. The type of behavior data that we collect must reflect the important feature of the behavior that we are trying to increase or decrease (e.g., frequency, rate, magnitude, latency, duration).

25. Should we collect "trial-by-trial" data during teaching?

Let's take the question back a step. What sort of data is necessary in order to make good, data-based decisions? If trial-by-trial data will be necessary to make the decisions, by all means collect trial-by-trial data. For example, you might want to trace the pattern of errors a student is making. Is the student performing incorrectly when you switch response requirements? Is he or she responding differently at the beginning of a block of trials? Is performance dropping off towards the end? Trial-by-trial data might be necessary to answer these sorts of questions.

26. What type of data collection should we use to measure the effectiveness of behavior management procedures?

Remember the answer to question 7: "it depends." You want to be able to ascertain whether or not your behavior treatment plan is having the desired effect. Consider the following anecdote. A new teacher and a Board Certified Behavior Analyst (B.C.B.A.) were working out a treatment plan to address the tantrums of a given student. The plan was set and the teacher went to carry out the plan with her classroom staff while the B.C.B.A. went to carry out a feeding program within the school. Later in the day, the B.C.B.A. came to the class to check on progress. He asked how the plan was affecting behavior. The reply came, "Well, I have good news and bad news. The good news is that he had only one tantrum. The bad news is that the tantrum lasted for four hours and two people are dead." The teacher was joking, of course, but the point is made. If the one tantrum had truly lasted for four hours, is frequency, the sheer number of occurrences, important? Of course not; in such a case we might look at duration of tantrum. If two people were truly dead, might we not do well to look at some measure of magnitude or severity? Perhaps the key issue is latency. How long was the student working before a tantrum was displayed? We must remain flexible and choose a measure that accurately reflects the important dimension of the behavior.

[As a personal side note, the teacher in question was possessed of a keen wit. We all went to a Bare Naked Ladies (BNL) concert at the Jones Beach Theater with some staff from the school (along with Meat Loaf, BNL gives the best concert you can possibly go to). Following the concert, the parking lot was quite backed up. I (BN) mentioned this fact and asked if anyone needed to use the bathroom before we got on the long line of cars. The reply was a biff to the back of the head, and a reminder that I was not out with students who needed to be prompted to use their verbal skills and a suggestion to give the B.C.B.A. thing a rest. If you're reading this Susan, give me a call. We miss you.]

27. Should we graph our data?

Yes, we believe that you should absolutely graph your data. The graphs provide a nice, pictorial representation of progress or lack thereof. Some of us are not really trained to process and analyze numbers in our heads. A Cartesian line graph will often hit you over the head, however, as it shows a flat line indicating no progress or an ascending or descending curve indicating behavioral movement (in the desired direction or otherwise).

We generally like for the staff member who conducted the session with the student to graph their own data. That is merely a convention, however. Some parents of home programs like to graph the data themselves. This allows the parent to continually monitor progress, and frees up the staff for more teaching time/tasks.

As a final note on the matter, we suggest keeping all the graphs in some sort of filing system. You never know when they will be necessary to show as a quick way of demonstrating progress (say at a committee meeting where funding is being discussed).

28. Should we hang onto the raw data once it is graphed?

The short answer here is yes, but don't get crazy. The raw data sheets can be important. It is only through those that you will see responding patterns (e.g., always gets the first item incorrect, but then gets items in a row correct until you change stimuli, etc.). That being said, the sheer number of sheets you will collect over time would fill a small silo. Adopt some sort of rule of thumb, such as that you'll keep raw data sheets for a month, unless otherwise specified. If progress is not occurring within a given program for one month, for example, it should certainly be revisited.

Chapter VI
Team Building

29. How many people on the team?

This is not a question that has a simple answer. A balance must be struck. Having too many people makes communication breakdowns more probable and staff training and meetings more difficult to arrange. Many instructors will also not commit to a program unless they are hired for a certain minimum number of hours per week. That will limit the number of individuals who can be hired.

On the other hand, having too few members may lead to its own difficulties. Burnout is common, as well as having a limited pool to choose from if someone must miss a session. As has been mentioned throughout, generalization must always be considered as well. Too few team members may limit some opportunities for generalization training.

30. What is the goal of staff training?

The goal of staff training is determined by the role that you expect the staff member to perform within the operation. Are you expecting the person to carry out programs that have been written by someone else (a "technician")? Are you expecting the person to make more active contributions to the data collection and programmatic design?

In an ideal world, we suggest that staff training should contain the following components, and staff should be trained to proficiency in each:

A. Information related to diagnosis and behavior commonly associated with the autistic-spectrum disorders.

B. Training regarding how to carry out the teaching procedures in use within the program.

C. Training regarding data collection procedures in use within the program.

D. Training regarding elements of functional analysis.

E. Training regarding behavior management procedures in use within the program.

F. Training regarding teaching procedures, data collection procedures, and behavior management procedures *not* currently in use within the program.

To create a technician, you need A and B and C (some would argue only B and C). For a more well-rounded staff member, you need all of the above. The way we often put it is that we are looking to indoctrinate a new staff member into the "culture" of ABA. The person has to understand the way behavior analysts think about behavior, the vocabulary they use, the assumptions they make regarding the lawfulness of behavior, and the general nature of data-based decision making. Beyond that, they must also become proficient in the actual techniques that have been created from this background.

A sad fact is that we must learn to rely on systems, not individuals. People come and go from programs, but the systems are what drive the process. This is why having someone stable "running the show" (generally the parent or hired consultant in a home program) is so important. The culture of the home program must be created, and then new staff members will simply fall into the culture as they are indoctrinated.

31. How do we introduce new staff members?

Staff training is a multiple-step process, and how involved it becomes is dependent upon one's goals (see previous question). Assuming that you want to have someone who will be an active, contributing member of the team, the new staff member will need some "classroom style" instruction regarding the autistic-spectrum disorders, teaching procedures, behavior management strategies, and data collection strategies. Current books should be read, and videos watched (see some suggestions in our reference section). If seminars regarding any of these topics offered by BCBA's are available in the local area, it is a very worthwhile investment of time and money. The new staff member should spend some time establishing him/herself as a reinforcer for the student during this time period, delivering noncontingent reinforcement and getting to know the student.

Following this pairing/introductory period, new staff members should be involved in an "apprenticeship" with more experienced staff members. We generally like this to be a "tag in and out" procedure. The new staff member stands/sits next to a more experienced staff member who is working on a given skill or conducting a given behavior management strategy. At some point, the new staff member "gets the tag" and the two change places. The new staff member now carries out the procedures, with the more experienced staff member sitting/standing by to deliver prompts (and hopefully lots of reinforcers!) to the new staff member. As the new staff member becomes more and more adept with the procedures, this teaming of staff can be gradually decreased. Time must be reserved for discussing the sessions away from the student. Much of what was learned in the introductory preparation may not make sense until the new staff member has begun to carry out procedures. In reality, (s)he may not know what questions to ask until (s)he has actually tried to carry out some of the procedures. For larger settings, this type of training may be carried out in a "pyramidal" style (for example, see Page, Iwata, and Reid, 1982).

It cannot be emphasized enough that all active staff members should attend professional conferences and read the journals of the field. There is simply no other way to stay current with the best data regarding the most effective means of teaching and behavior management. This is an ever-expanding field, and we can never rest on the past.

32. Should we use related service providers?

This is something of a controversial question within applied behavior analytic circles. Many schools within the ABA tradition reason that behavior is just that, behavior. We have many empirically-validated techniques for teaching a wide variety of behavior. Why should talking or movement receive special consideration? For this reason, many schools within the ABA tradition have avoided the use of related service providers. No special consideration is given for speech therapy or occupational therapy, for example, and such providers are not employed within the programs. At least one report found that adding such providers to a school-based teaching team did not lead to faster acquisition of skills by students (Needelman, 2000).

There is a danger here, however. In a prior work I (Newman, 2002) recounted an event that occurred when I was asked to come in and provide a new set of eyes for a home program. A friend of mine was a speech therapist on the team. She had asked me to come in due to her concern regarding some of the suggestions being made by the consultant overseeing the home program. At one point, she modeled a mand for the student, who was asking for "juice." "Duh duh duh juice," she modeled.

I assumed that this was one of the odd things the consultant had recommended. When I asked her about it, she nonchalantly mentioned that "duh" was a sound that typically came in before "juh" and was both easier to produce and mastery of that skill would make it easier to work towards the more correct pronunciation. I realized that while I had previously taught many students to request juice, I could have been more efficient with the knowledge of typical development of sound production.

Does this mean that speech therapists and similar professionals need to carry out daily sessions with the students? To be honest, we don't feel that this is the most constructive use of the time of professionals who are in very short supply. Where we come from, related service providers such as speech therapists have three functions:

A. They diagnose any problems that their unique training allows them to diagnose.

B. They design programs and strategies to address those deficits.

C. They train everyone else to carry out those programs and strategies.

This consultative model gets you the most "bang for the buck." When parents come to our schools for intake, they are often very concerned about how many times a given related service, say speech therapy, is on the IEP. We answer that we are not overly concerned with this issue. The speech therapist may do his/her thing during three scheduled 30 minute sessions during the week, but that's a drop in the bucket compared to the number of times the exact same programs will be carried out by a teacher and a number of teacher assistants that have been trained to carry out the programs in the same way by that same speech therapist. As is the case with other programming, speech and other related service programs must be data-based and carefully designed and monitored using principles of ABA (see Chapter II, Question #13).

33. Who should work on which programs?

That has a simple answer - *everyone* should do *everything*. There is no such thing as a "speech therapist program" or an "occupational therapist program." If a skill is important enough for anyone to work on, it is important enough for everyone to work on.

Beyond this simple precept, the general concept of *failure to generalize* must be appreciated. As alluded to previously, very few students diagnosed with autism spontaneously generalize their skills across individuals, stimuli, or phrasing of instructions. Generalization cannot simply be hoped for, it must be programmed for. That means having a number of people involved in the teaching and maintenance effort.

We take this extremely seriously. To reach mastery on a given skill, the criteria we use specifies that at least two instructors have carried out the program and received sufficiently high scores. If only one instructor were working on a program, therefore, mastery criteria would never be reached.

34. What is the decision-making hierarchy?

Generally speaking, there is a specific person or persons responsible for designing programming (both skill acquisition and decreasing competing behavior). Programming is designed by this person or persons and then introduced to the other staff members.

The most highly trained person is generally responsible for designing programming. The programming, however, is dependent upon data collected by *everyone*. ABA is the most egalitarian of enterprises. Everyone's data holds equal weight, as long as it is properly collected. These data guide all of the decision-making (see Chapter V on Data Collection).

This being said, parental input is also vital. In some cases, the parent and the programmer are one and the same. More often, the parent has brought in outside help to guide the programmatic effort. Regardless, parental input is a crucial concern. What the parent regards as a priority, and what (s)he regards as an acceptable procedure, will vary. If the parent does not agree with a particular program or approach, follow-through will be absent and progress in the disputed area will not be forthcoming. Therefore, cooperation and eventual agreement is vital. If a programmer does not agree with parental decisions, (s)he has the ethical responsibility to voice concerns, hopefully citing clinical literature and data as opposed to mere opinion. If agreement can still not be reached, the Behavior Analyst Certification Board (www.BACB.com) has guidelines for how such professional relationships should be terminated.

35. Should we have team meetings?

You should have team meetings only if you want to see progress. In all seriousness, it is next to impossible to assure consistent programming without frequent team meetings. Everyone needs to get around the table and go through the program book to ensure that everyone is carrying out the procedures and collecting the data consistently. Without consistent data collection, the vital information to guide the decision-making process will be flawed. Programming will then be flawed, which can have very serious implications when dealing with behavior such as self-injury, aggression, or running away.

At team meetings, instructors need to watch and provide feedback regarding video-taped sessions and/or live examples. Without such meetings, "drift" is inevitable. Teaching and data collection procedures break down, and the last thing you want is "everyone doing their own thing." Generalization is one thing, chaos is another.

36. How do we resolve clinical disagreements?

Disagreements regarding how teaching and behavior management should proceed must be resolved in an objective, data-based manner. This should not be a matter of authority, or personality, or even who is most experienced. In real life of course, frequently the team leader is most experienced or has the most advanced degree. This should be reflected in the degree to which the person suggests how to collect careful and meaningful data and uses the existing clinical literature, and not just a matter of the person pulling rank. (Personal note: Of course, we'd be lying if we said we didn't sometimes feel like simply following Jennica's playful suggestion that we send all the antagonists out to play paintball.)

Chapter VII

Program Books

37. What sections should be in the program book?

We generally recommend the following sections:

    A.   An assessments section (reinforcer inventories, a copy of the current Individualized Education Program (IEP), statements of skills and deficits, etc.).

    B.   Current programs (raw data sheets and descriptions of how to carry out programs).

    C.   Generalization programs.

    D.   Maintenance programs.

    E.   Graphs.

    F.   Progress notes.

Please *do* pay attention to the progress notes section. Do not, under penalty of torture, write "Jim had a good day." Be descriptive. Describe skills that reached mastery criterion during the session, or were just performed really well. Note any difficult programs. Note any idiosyncratic responding patterns (e.g., "he seemed to be picking the choice on the right more frequently than not"). Note general appearance. Was the student lethargic or energetic? Was he laughing or crying for no obvious reason? Did any particular consequences function really well as reinforcers, or were any previously-established reinforcers duds today? The progress notes are often ignored, but they can provide us with information that may not be immediately obvious from the numbers.

38. How many programs?

There is no hard and fast answer here. There are a variety of factors that you need to take into account when selecting programs. Is each program being worked through each day? If not, there may be too many programs. Is the student making expected progress with each program? If not, one potential reason is that the skill needs to be practiced more frequently (again, too many programs?). On the other hand, are each of the crucial areas we mentioned in the beginning of Chapter II being addressed? If not, there may be crucial programs missing and, in all probability, these skills will not develop spontaneously. In this latter case, the missing programmatic areas will obviously have to be added in.

On my (DR) very memorable trip to Northern Ireland with Bobby one year, I had the fortune to meet an appealing little boy who was having great difficulty with his home program. According to his mum, the little guy was making no progress and was becoming increasingly frustrated, non-compliant, and aggressive. When I asked her to show me what they were working on, she demonstrated a simple gross motor imitation drill – "Do this" followed by a hand clap. OK, I said, let's see what else – and the mother reported that their consultant told them that he'd have to master THIS program before working on anything else at all. So the poor child (and his poor mother) spent hours a day doing ONE program with ONE step in it, and it wasn't even functional. How surprising is it that they would both be frustrated and bored with the home program? Here's a definite answer to the questions of how many programs – more than one!

Generally speaking, we recommend beginning with a few simple programs and adding in more as programming becomes more smooth and efficient. When you have worked up to the double digits, though, make sure to constantly assess if each program is truly addressing a necessary area.

39. Should we "skip around" in the book?

Read Question #7 and say it with us: "it depends!" As a general rule, skipping around while performing intensive teaching tasks is an excellent idea. We want the student to attend to each instruction, which means that each new instruction must be worth attending to. If you keep repeating the same instruction over and over, you run the risk of becoming noise. The student doesn't actually have to listen to what you are saying. (S)he merely has to hear the sound of the adult voice ("wah wah wah wah" like the adults in the Charlie Brown cartoons) and generally performs whatever movement was reinforced last. Failure to skip around may create a situation wherein the student can only perform the skill if he warms up through repeated trials first (e.g. he does whatever he received a reinforcer for last time, then gets it wrong when you switch requests until you prompt the new response.) Failure to skip around can also get really boring and lead to competing behavior.

Chapter VIII

Helping a Child to Become a Willing Learner

40. What is compliance training?

Compliance training refers to the development of *instructional control*. In other words, when an instruction is delivered, the individual tends to do what was asked. This is sometimes referred to as a response class of instruction following.

Compliance training begins with reinforcement. The instructor provides an instruction in the form of some verbal or visual cue (or a combination of the two) and delivers a reinforcing consequence when the individual complies with the request. One can "stack the deck" towards success by beginning with requests only for skills already well within the student's behavioral capabilities. Additionally, use reinforcers that are unavailable to the child except through compliance with the instructor (see the description, for example, in Sundberg and Partington, 1998). Gradually, one increases the difficulty of the behaviors requested, all the while keeping up high levels of reinforcement. These will also be gradually thinned over time. Don't thin too quickly, however, or you will not be offering enough reinforcement and inadvertently put the desired behavior on extinction.

Clinicians disagree on the extent to which they recommend "following the child's lead" in conducting compliance training. Each side makes a valid point. Chances of compliance will be increased, and competing behavior made less probable, if you work around the student's motivation. Those on the other side point out that there is nothing particularly natural about the world following you around, looking for naturally occurring motivating conditions. In school, for example, you are expected to follow a teacher's directions, given simultaneously to the entire class, without regard to your individual motivation. If we don't teach students to comply with instructions under such circumstances, we have failed programmatically.

So what is the answer? As so often is the case, go back to the basic rules of "assume nothing" and "it depends". A student needs to learn to follow directions, even if (s)he is not particularly motivated to do so. A combination may therefore be the most prudent course. Begin compliance training under the motivating condition, and gradually introduce the "because I need you to comply whether you're happy about it or not" instructions as instructional control develops and chances of compliance with these instructions increases.

When one has begun to provide instructions that simply must be followed, regardless of the motivational state of the student, it is important to stack the deck. Only make requests once, and follow through until the student complies with the request. Use prompting procedures as necessary to ensure compliance (e.g., Lovaas, 2003). Do not make requests if you are not in a position to follow through and ensure completion of the request by the student, or you run a serious risk of undermining compliance training (Leaf & McEachin, 1999). Finally, don't forget to have some form of reinforcement available for the student when compliance is achieved.

41. How should we set up for a session?

When a session is due to begin, make sure that the arrival of the interventionist does *not* signal that fun is coming to an end. If anything, strive for the opposite effect. The arrival of the interventionist should mean that the fun is just beginning. Remember, you want the student to be motivated to engage with the therapist, not to have to peel the child off mom's leg and carry him away kicking and screaming. In order to avoid setting the therapist up as the "killjoy," make sure that on-going fun is terminated several minutes prior to the therapist's arrival. There should not be a favorite video playing, for example, which will be turned off when the therapist arrives. Mom and Dad should not be engaging in reinforcing rough-housing or pretend play that comes to a screeching, grinding halt with the arrival of the therapist. Finally, the therapist should be prepared to spend several minutes engaging in reinforcing activities with the child when first arriving.

42. What if the child has trouble separating from a parent for teaching?

If a child has trouble separating from a parent to begin work, there are various strategies that can be attempted. The simplest, although least pleasant, is to have the parent simply disappear. Any tantrums that ensue will extinguish if the parent does not reappear in response to the tantrum and if the activities of the teaching session are appropriately reinforcing. A more pleasant strategy is to have the parent present, and to involve the parent in activities if at all possible. The parent can then begin to fade away during sessions, first "going out to get something" and returning a few seconds later. These comings and goings can become more and more frequent and of longer and longer duration. It is important that the parent does not return until the child is engaging in appropriate behavior in order to avoid reinforcing the problem behavior. Third, access to parent can be used as a reinforcer, using a token economy for example.

Chapter IX

Preparing to Teach

43. How do we make sure we're not missing anything?

There's a simple answer to this one, a reminder to ASSUME NOTHING! A great many students diagnosed with autistic-spectrum disorders are characterized as displaying atypical development. Therefore, learning is rarely uniform and rarely follows a typical developmental sequence. "Splinter skills," which are highly developed skills in particular areas, are often present. The presence of those skills, however, does not guarantee that other skills, even if they might intuitively seem to be simpler, are present. In other words, just because a student can tell you every stop on the New York City subway system, and every train that connects at every stop, that does not mean that he is able to perform two column addition, or can appropriately return a greeting or dress appropriately for the weather.

Similarly, many behaviors that seem to be the same are actually quite different. Being able to point to the color red upon request is a different skill than being able to verbally name it when red is presented. The fact that a student is able to perform a given skill while sitting 1 on 1 with an instructor does not mean that (s)he is able to perform that same skill while sitting in a group. Being able to touch your nose in response to a visual model and "do this" is different from being able to touch your nose in response to the verbal request to "touch your nose."

Consider these three different questions:

A. "Would you like a drink?"

B. "Is your name Erin?"

C. "Is the car black?"

On the surface, these are all "yes and no" questions. Closer examination, however, shows that they are actually quite different. The first is a question regarding a personal want. The second question asks for an evaluation of personal information. The third refers to a fact in the environment. These are actually very different questions, and require very different pre-requisite skills. Please revisit our discussion of this topic in Chapter II, Questions #8 and #9 before moving on.

44.   What are pre-requisite skills?

Pre-requisite skills are those skills that the student must have previously mastered before (s)he can acquire a skill currently being targeted. For example, the ability to scan an array of stimuli placed on a table may be considered a pre-requisite skill for receptive object identification. The ability to point or otherwise indicate (upon request) which stimulus is the correct one would also be considered a pre-requisite skill to receptive object identification. Limited progress is made and learners often become frustrated when being expected to complete a task before they acquire the pre-requisite skills necessary for that task.

45. Should we conduct a programmatic baseline?

Yes. Anyone who wants to tell you that they can provide programming for a given student without first assessing the student's existing skills is selling something. Time will be wasted on working on skills the student already has, or the student will be frustrated by working on programs that are not appropriate to his/her skill level. It is important to remember that individualization is the key to behavioral programming.

For a really nice example of this, see Bourret, Vollmer, & Rapp (2004) from the ever-reliable *Journal of Applied Behavior Analysis*. Bourret and colleagues noted that while mand training procedures are described within the research literature, exactly how to decide which procedure to apply is often lacking. By conducting careful baselines, they were able to show how to match procedure to student skill level for maximum teaching efficiency.

46. How do we conduct a baseline?

There are different schools of thought on this issue. Some people like to conduct a baseline by testing students' skills without providing reinforcement or feedback. They simply ask the student to perform particular skills and assess accuracy.

Personally, we like to conduct baseline under the same conditions as those under which teaching will be conducted (i.e., including reinforcement for correct responses and feedback on incorrect responding). While this may not be technically correct, and while it is true that "teaching" may be taking place during baseline, is this the crucial issue? We are attempting to ascertain the student's skill levels. If I do not provide reinforcement for correct responding, might I accidentally be extinguishing correct responding? If I do provide feedback for incorrect responding, the data will reflect the inability of the student to perform the skill correctly the first time and teaching levels will be adjusted accordingly.

47. Should we always give the child access to things when (s)he asks for them?

It is true that we should reinforce appropriate manding, especially for students who are in the beginning stages of learning how to express their needs and wants appropriately. In our ABA programming, however, we have to refer to the sobering reminder from the Rolling Stones: you can't always get what you want. For a student who has difficulty accepting "no," we can gradually shape the student's ability to tolerate not getting what (s)he wants. Initially, when the student asks for a chip for the tenth time, we might say "You can't have a chip, but you can have a pretzel." The student is able to access another preferred item, just not the one they asked for. Eventually, after several intermediate steps, the student may be told something like "No, maybe later." Likewise, we can shape the student's ability to wait appropriately by gradually increasing the duration of time before the student accesses the item or activity after being told to "wait."

When teaching students to tolerate "no" or to wait appropriately, it is important to collect the appropriate data to measure the student's ability to tolerate each step before moving on to the next, more difficult step. Most importantly, the student should still be able to access the requested item or activity without a delay for the majority of mands in order to prevent extinction of manding behavior.

Chapter X
Getting Teaching Right

48. Where should teaching be conducted?

Before all is said and done, teaching must be conducted *everywhere*. As mentioned above, it is unfortunately more often the rule than the exception that students diagnosed with autism do not generalize acquired skills. Therefore, we have to deliberately program for generalization. We cannot simply wish, hope, or even pray for it.

That being said, it is true that many students diagnosed with autism have a great deal of trouble focusing on relevant stimuli and are extremely easily distracted. It has therefore been a great temptation, and it can indeed be very effective, to create a specific teaching setting. This is where the stereotype originates of the small table and chairs where teaching is *always* conducted.

It is true that some students do require this segregated setting in order to *begin* to learn effectively. If teaching remains in this setting, however, it is unlikely that skills will generalize. Many programmers seem to fail to appreciate this fact, so please understand the occasional lack of social skills (shown by one of our authors):

Programmer: "Here are our teaching table and chairs!"

Bobby: "Good, now let's burn them!"

Of course we don't need to burn them, and in fact we might need to use them (at least temporarily). A plan must always be in place for how and when we are going to be begin working away from this isolated setting.

49. Should we begin with "isolated" or "randomized" material?

Refer back to Chapter I, Question #7. Now say it with us, "it depends." Let's begin with some definitions. To work on a single skill in isolation refers to working on it repeatedly, without mixing in other directions. To work on a skill randomly (in randomization) refers to mixing up the requests, mixing in other targets within the same program or mixing in other programs.

Many students require you to begin working on a skill in isolation in order to ensure the success and reinforcement that will make the sessions reinforcing and encourage learning. Once two targets or skills have been mastered in isolation, they can then be mixed into the random rotation. At any given time, any given program might have one or two targets being acquired in isolation and several previously mastered targets that are being practiced in randomization.

Be careful when providing such teaching in isolation, however, as it is possible to reinforce bad habits. When a student has "mastered" a skill in isolation, has (s)he truly learned it? Is it possible that the student is just repeating the last behavior that (s)he received a reinforcer for performing? Are we possibly teaching students *not* to listen, as the next instruction will simply be the same as the last one? For this reason, we often introduce two steps from the very beginning for children who may be demonstrating such learning difficulties. Acquisition may be slower, but we will not be digging a hole for ourselves and the student. By introducing the two steps simultaneously, the student will have no choice but to learn to attend to the instruction in order to perform the skill correctly.

Another way to avoid the risk of teaching the student to just repeat the last behavior emitted is to intersperse trials of previously mastered targets with trials of the new target. As well as "getting the student's mind off" the most recently emitted behavior, this helps to reduce frustration for the learner by providing "easy" trials and takes advantage of behavioral momentum (see Davis, Brady, Williams & Hamilton, 1992).

50. Should we reinforce "prompted trials?"

To examine this issue, let's first establish what we mean by a "prompt." A prompt, in this case, is something *above and beyond* the ordinary instruction that is used to occasion a behavior. An example might be a physical prompt to perform a motor skill that accompanies a verbal direction.

So then, if the student requires this additional prompt to perform the skill, do we reinforce or not? Generally speaking, we would not reinforce a prompted trial as heavily as we would reinforce an independently performed skill. There are times, however, when a specific level of prompting is written into the teaching procedure. We often do this when a particular skill is not being acquired easily. A prompting system is put into place, and a response that occurs *within our current level of prompting* is certainly eligible for reinforcement. We would not want to reinforce responses that require more than our current level of prompting, however.

51. Should we end a block of trials on a prompted response?

We would prefer not to do this. Whenever a student has required an additional prompt in order to perform a skill correctly, it is a good idea to allow him/her to then have the opportunity to perform the skill independently. It is always a good idea to seek to end a work period with the student enjoying a successful experience. Have him/her perform the skill or the closest approximation possible and reinforce!

52. What is this talk about "responses" versus "concepts"?

This idea can best be explained by example. Suppose one student is taught "nose" in a body-part identification drill by being taught to touch his nose. Another student is taught "nose" by being prompted to touch his nose, the interventionist's nose, and the nose of a stuffed animal. Consider colors. One student is taught "red" with a red piece of construction paper. Another student is taught with red construction paper, crayons, markers, paints, and toy cars. Who do you suppose will generalize the *concept* more easily?

By teaching in this more concept-based way, you will have a student who will understand what noses are, rather than thinking that only the bump on *his* face is called nose. He'll know what red is, rather than thinking that the piece of paper is named red.

Of course, we have to repeat our refrain. Applied Behavior Analytic instruction is a data-based discipline. The data you collect guide the teaching process. How many exemplars you can include, and how quickly you introduce them, will vary by student and you must adjust teaching accordingly. Some students will need to begin with relatively few (or one) exemplars. Others can have many exemplars and work on the more general concept earlier.

53. Should we work on receptive and expressive targets together?

While this is commonly done, we recommend against it. Often, the targets are combined by, for example, asking the student to point to the color blue. Following this, the interventionist will point to the stimulus and say "what color?"

We suggest avoiding this practice, as you may inadvertently be giving extra "hints" for the expressive target via conducting the receptive target first. In other words, the word "blue" is still in the air from your previous request when you then ask "what color?" Teaching skills in this way may teach the student a bad habit. Rather than looking in the environment for the correct answer, the student learns to simply attempt to repeat prior utterances from the interventionist.

Of course, as we have previously indicated, one cannot assume that any skill will develop if one does not specifically target and teach it. Therefore, it will be necessary to target both receptive and expressive skills. We simply recommend that you break up the teaching by interspersing other requests. To cite the prior example, you can work on "blue" as a receptive target. Following this receptive target, however, we recommend interspersing trials of another skill prior to expressive color identification for "blue."

54. How do we select teaching stimuli?

Teaching stimuli must be chosen carefully so that they accurately reflect the concept you are trying to teach, and only that concept. Consider the "comparative concepts" sub-program called "short and long," and a teacher who was planning to use a wooden yardstick to teach long, and a foot-long plastic ruler to teach short.

The teaching stimuli chosen for this program are fatally flawed. The student may indeed learn to touch the yardstick for "long," and the ruler for "short." But does the student actually have the concept? There is no way to know. Perhaps the student thinks long means "made of wood" or "brown." Perhaps short, to this student means "red," or "made of plastic." The stimuli vary according to too many dimensions for clear teaching.

When a student is having trouble in this sort of program, frequently it is the teaching stimuli we must consider. Students can sometimes be quite "overselective," meaning that they attend only to one particular aspect of a stimulus and not necessarily the important one. Consider a student who is trying to learn the difference between different denominations of currency by looking at the color of the paper, or the size of the paper, or the presence of a picture in the middle of the bill. Of course, this will not work. Those dimensions are exactly the same for all U.S. bills. The student must learn to pay attention to the relevant detail, the number in the corners.

Stimuli in such discrimination programs should generally be exactly the same, except for the dimension you are trying to teach. When things are not going well, it is often a detective game to figure out why. A particular student was not doing well with a "bigger and smaller" program. He scored 100% when the larger and smaller Tigger toys from Winnie the Pooh used to teach the original discrimination were used. When other items were introduced however, performance was random. So why could he tell bigger and smaller with the Tiggers, but not with the other stimuli? The answer is simple; he couldn't. The Tiggers differed in a dimension no one but the student had noticed: the smaller Tigger was sitting, and the larger Tigger was standing (or bouncing, more likely). He selected not by size, but by body position. When other stimuli were introduced that did not vary by this dimension, performance deteriorated. Thus, it is important to carefully select teaching stimuli to capture the dimension we want to teach, minimize unrelated dimensions, and to teach using multiple exemplars.

55. How many SD's?

In keeping with our previous discussion regarding generalization, there are two schools of thought here. Should we begin with one SD (e.g., "what's your name?") and then generalize to other instructions, or should we begin teaching with multiple alternate phrasings of the question?

As we stated above, we lean towards teaching with multiple alternate SD's. By teaching with only one phrasing, the student may not actually be ready for real-world applications. People he runs into may not know that they have to phrase the question "what's your name" as opposed to "what's your *first* name" or "who are you" or "what do they call you," etc. Consider a student who works on colors with the phrase "*touch* <u>color</u>." Suppose someone then says "*give me* <u>color</u>" or "*point to* <u>color</u>" or "*show me* <u>color</u>" or "*which one is* <u>color</u>?" We learned an expression from Dr. Steve Gallagher in Northern Ireland. "You have two hopes, no hope and Bob Hope."

As always, we repeat the mantra. Let the data guide the decision-making process. If the student is not showing mastery with the multiple phrasings, back it down to fewer or simpler phrasings and then build back up when mastery is achieved.

56. What sorts of prompting strategies should we use?

The two factors to take into consideration are:

      A. What works for the student?

      B. What stimuli will be available in everyday life?

To take a common example, a student may learn very well with spoken cues, or may learn better with visual cue strategies. Consider that much of the instruction we typically receive in the everyday world consists of spoken cues and information. Some cues are visual, however, and we need to be able to attend to these as well. As with other skill areas, we begin where the student is and work our way to where we need to be. To continue the example, if a student performs particularly well with visual cue strategies, we may begin with these and gradually fade in the more auditory cues. Similarly, if the student attends to the auditory cues, but not the visual ones, we might begin with the auditory cues and fade in visual ones (or at least teach how to follow specific visual cues such as hallway signs and traffic signals).

Whatever cues are being used, there must always be a plan in place for fading any extra cues/prompts back towards the ordinary cues of everyday life. If we do not do this, we run the risk of creating "prompt dependency" and having the student be unable to function independently in everyday life. There is an entire literature on prompt-fading (e.g., "most to least" versus "least to most") and the programmer must plan accordingly. Far too many students don't move unless literally provided with a physical push in the right direction. This is generally the result of poor physical prompt fading.

When attempting to teach discriminations between stimuli, additional prompting is often needed. Consider a $5.00 bill and a $10.00 bill. Each has a monochromatic portrait in the same place. They are the same shape, the same size, the same color. They have numbers and circles in the same places. They are alike in many ways, and differ in only a few. You are asking the student with autism to ignore all the ways in which they are the same and to only hone in on the few ways they are different. This may be impossible for some students who are characterized as "overselective" in their responding. For the student to be able to make the discrimination, you may have to make the bills more dissimilar. One way is through *stimulus superimposition*, such as coloring in the "5's" in red. This should help the student make the distinction. Of course, in real life $5.00 bills don't come in red.

Therefore, you will need to use a fading procedure. Each day, almost imperceptibly, you would begin coloring in the numbers lighter and lighter, or perhaps coloring in less and less of the total area. Through the use of a skillful fading procedure, the student will be able to continue to make the discrimination even after fading has progressed to the point where no additional coloring is added.

57. How many trials in a block (how much practice)?

There's an easy answer to this one. Do as many trials as you need to do to help the student learn the skill. There is nothing magical about the number ten, and in our darker moments we have suggested that the only reason to do ten trials is an inability to calculate percentages in anything other than 10's. If that happens to be the case for anyone you know, we'll arrange to have someone buy the person a calculator as a holiday present, or at least provide a percentage finder sheet.

Do as many trials as are necessary. If a student gets the first five correct, why beat it to death and risk decrements or competing behavior due to boredom? If a student seems to be demonstrating increased accuracy after a period of random responding, why not take advantage of the behavioral momentum and do a few more?

58. Should we teach eye contact?

Eye to face contact is an important skill. Someone who is able to see but does not look at others when listening will certainly be considered odd by the population at large. Similarly, a person who does not look at others while they are speaking may miss crucial information related to body language and facial expressions. This

68

may make social interaction difficult (Klin, Jones, Schultz, Volkmar, & Cohen, 2002).

It therefore follows that we recommend teaching eye contact as a skill. That does *not* necessarily mean drilling eye contact as its own program, however. One can work on eye contact while working on another program (e.g., object discrimination). Consider the two alternatives:

A. "Look at me" is followed either by reinforcing if the student looks at the interventionist, or a corrective prompt if (s)he does not. A second eye contact trial is then performed.

B. "Look at me" is followed either by reinforcing if the student looks at the interventionist, or a corrective prompt if she does not. Once the eye contact is established and reinforced, however, the interventionist immediately provides an instruction such as "do this" accompanied by a motor action. The student now has the opportunity to earn reinforcement for appropriate imitation. (Please note that data are kept for the eye contact just as it would be if it were its own drill. Both the eye contact and object discrimination data sheets are available to the interventionist simultaneously).

With the latter strategy, eye contact is placed in the context of an interaction, rather than two people just looking at each other silently, for its own sake. In this sense, it is more of a functional skill, and establishing eye contact becomes a step in the chain towards earning additional reinforcement. While some students might need to begin with Strategy A, we would hope to move towards Strategy B as soon as possible. Remember to keep up on requiring eye contact whenever interacting, not just when collecting data.

Try not to inadvertently encourage inappropriate behavior. Drilling eye contact that does *not* lead to an additional interaction could be doing just that. In everyday life, do you ask someone to look at you, and then just stare at them without any further comment or interaction? Probably not, unless you are attempting some form of stage hypnotism or are a member of the Manson family. Forgive the somewhat shocking reference, but we wish to highlight just how odd it can appear to simply stare at someone with no further meaningful exchange. Remember that we are attempting to help people with autism to engage in meaningful interaction, and not to appear socially strange. Someone who stares without further follow-up *will* appear socially peculiar.

As an additional note on this matter, do not forget about the power of simple shaping. When first beginning programming, a response definition for an appropriate response by the student (for example, a verbal imitation) might not include that eye contact was maintained while the verbalization was made. In later programming, eye contact would be required while responding in order for the response to be reinforced.

Chapter XI

Communication Goals

59. How do we establish functional language as soon as possible?

Learning to communicate can be particularly difficult for students diagnosed with autistic-spectrum disorders. For this reason, it is important that the language skills being taught will help students to negotiate their world as soon as possible. This might mean working on the student being able to make a particular sound that will function as an approximation to a mand rather than working on the same sound as a pure vocal imitation (echoic) that is separated from any functional communication context. For a really nice example of this in action, see Arntzen and Almas (2002), and the differences found when attempting to teach only via a labeling (tacting) training procedure, versus a mand-tact procedure. Teaching under the more motivating requesting condition led to faster acquisition of language. This is not to say, of course, that one would never work on a pure vocal imitation or labeling skill.

When teaching a student to mand, we have to always remember to use items that have been established as reinforcing *at this moment*. Don't expect the person to mand for a cookie after just finishing a five course meal. In general, try to take advantage of establishing operations and teach early language under the most motivating conditions possible. Keeping these things in mind when teaching functional language will make the student better able to negotiate the world as quickly as possible.

60. Should we teach in two languages?

Generally speaking, this is not a good idea. Typically developing children can be exposed to two languages and, while a bit delayed in both, will generally wind up becoming bi-lingual and still within the normal range. Throw in a language disability, however, and all bets are off. The student will usually have enough difficulty in acquiring just one language. Throwing two languages at the student may make it difficult for him/her to acquire functional fluency in either.

The bottom line here is to pick one language. That should be the language of instruction in program, as well as the language spoken at home. It is silly for us to work on "cat" at school and have it be called "gato" at home, or vice versa. Which language should be chosen is a matter of what is most functional for the student.

61. Should we teach augmentative communication strategies?

This is an area of professional controversy. On one side are those who suggest that teaching an augmentative communication strategy such as sign language or picture exchange will cut down on the motivation for the student to put in the effort necessary to learn to speak. Why should he go through the effort if making some hand gestures can get wants and needs met? On the other hand are clinicians who ask "what would your day be like if you couldn't mand?" (Sundberg, 2004). Suppose we avoid teaching an augmentative communication strategy while we work on the development of speech. A great many behavioral difficulties may arise if the individual has no means of indicating wants or needs, not even able to indicate pain (e.g., Carr & Durand, 1985).

While the data are still open to interpretation, many clinicians have come down on the side of teaching the augmentative communication system and do not believe that it hampers acquisition of speaking (e.g., a literature review by Barr Berotti, et al., 2004). At any rate, augmentative communication can be combined with spoken language. As vocal approximations shape up through mand and verbal imitation training, for example, these can be combined with sign or picture symbols. The symbol card or sign would insufficient unless accompanied by a vocalization by the student. As the vocalization becomes more clear, the picture symbol or sign usage would be faded.

Chapter XII

The Importance of Teaching
Life Relevant Skills

62. Should we conduct toilet training?

As a personal bias, we like to work on this skill as soon as possible. Generally speaking, it is not a very difficult skill to teach if the student is sufficiently physically developed. Therefore, it is not terribly time-consuming to do.

The benefits of toilet-training are immediate and highly valuable. Families will be tremendously relieved of a time, financial, and physical burden. Furthermore, students who are toilet trained are generally easier to teach. It is not necessary to interrupt programmatic activities to change diapers. Additionally, people tend to think of students who are toilet trained as higher-functioning than students who are not, regardless of other skills that have been developed. It may not be fair, but there it is. Finally, failure to be toilet trained may greatly interfere with placement in less restrictive settings, and may expose the student to condescension from peers.

63. Should we teach leisure skills?

The answer to this one is an emphatic YES. While this area is often under-emphasized, it should not be. Consider the issue of the Dead Man's Test discussed later in Chapter XVI, Question #98. Simply because I help a student to stop engaging in inappropriate behavior does not mean that (s)he will spontaneously develop appropriate behavior in its place. The most intensive learning schedule in the world is still going to leave the student with considerable down-time. If I do not teach the student how to constructively engage him/herself during that alone time, it is unlikely that (s)he will be appropriately engaged. Idle hands are the devil's workshop and all like that.

This issue aside, teaching appropriate leisure skills can be crucial for improved family functioning. Mother and father need to be able to be on the telephone for five minutes without wondering if their child is engaged in aimless or destructive behavior. Putting it even more bluntly, we all have to go to the bathroom at some point.

On a more esoteric level, this is a fundamental quality of life issue. We all have our hobbies. We develop our interests, and we must encourage the student to do the same. Few things are more normalizing for family life. Just to give a few examples, preschoolers might be taught to play with play-doh, color, and stack blocks. School-age children could learn to put together puzzles, look through magazines, jump rope, shoot baskets, and play computer or video games. Teenagers can put together model cars, jog, lift weights or dance, play paddleball, surf the internet (with supervision), and needlepoint.

64. Should we teach self-help skills?

Following a logic similar to that laid out above regarding toilet training, self-help skills (e.g, dressing, feeding) should absolutely be targeted. In fact, we would argue that in most cases they are not targeted often enough or early enough. In view of our ongoing theme about the Right to Effective Treatment, the student has the right to expect that the instructor will use the most effective means available to help the individual to increase his/her autonomy. That certainly means teaching self-help skills. If no other reason seems compelling, simply consider the personal dignity involved in being able to take care of one's own feeding or hygiene needs.

There is also still the issue that individuals outside the student's immediate social circle will put a high premium on self-help skills. Regardless of other skills that have been developed by the student, the obvious absence of self-help skills will lead outsiders to think of the student as more impaired than if (s)he had these skills. It may not be fair, but it is the reality.

65. Should we teach household skills?

There's a simple answer to this one, also. Is the student a member of the family? If so, then (s)he should pitch in with the chores of everyday living, the same as everyone else. The same subtle psychology of functioning levels applies here, as well as the discussions of personal dignity mentioned at the outset. Such skills are often easily taught through basic shaping, chaining and task analysis (see Chapter III for a description of these essential concepts).

Chapter XIII

Reinforcers

66. How are reinforcers defined?

A reinforcer is a consequence that, when it is provided following a given behavior, makes that behavior more likely in the future. Please note the most important aspect of this definition: not every consequence is a reinforcer, despite all good intentions. If you provide a given consequence after a given behavior, and there is no observed increase in the future probability of that behavior, then that consequence is *not* a reinforcer. The consequence might be neutral (no effect), or it might even be a punisher (decreasing future probability of the specific behavior).

It is important to realize is that reinforcement has nothing to do with what you intended to have happen when you delivered the given consequence. We sometimes accidentally reinforce behavior, for example, by showing a reaction for a given behavior without realizing that it is this reaction that is maintaining the behavior (e.g., saying "no yelling" when a student is engaging in yelling that serves an attention-seeking function). This is why a great deal of the real activity of behavior analysis entails discovering what reinforcers may inadvertently be maintaining behavior. On the flip side, just because a consequence seems like it will be a reinforcer, or even was a reinforcer in the past or for a different behavior, does not mean that it will be a reinforcer under the current circumstances. For example, the toy that was so motivating yesterday may not be interesting at all to a child today.

As a final consideration, note that reinforcers must be defined only in terms of their effect on behavior (i.e., increasing the probability of the behavior). We should not speak of an individual "liking" the consequence. That can lead us up a blind alley. If an individual is more likely to engage in the behavior in question (e.g., throwing items) if throwing leads to his being yelled at, then being yelled at is functioning as a reinforcer. He may not "like" being yelled at, but the yelling is serving as a reinforcer.

67. What sorts of reinforcers should we use?

The answer to this one is easy: use whatever works! Some people have difficulty, for example, with using edible reinforcers. In our opinion, this is a bit short-sighted. Some students begin intervention with a very narrow range of reinforcers. In other words, edibles may be all that is effective. Skillful pairing of edibles with other potential reinforcers, however, will lead to the other consequences (including instructor praise) becoming reinforcers. To avoid the use of a particular consequence, however, on the grounds that you don't like the way it looks is short-sighted and may be self-defeating. I (BN) worked with a student who found it reinforcing to throw water on me. What do I care? It's not like I have any dignity, anyway. It served to get him interested in interacting, and then we shaped it into more appropriate water gun play, which we then generalized to peers, etc.

As a short-hand, we recommend breaking down the various types of positive reinforcers as follows:

A. Primary reinforcers: these you are born with and do not need to learn to find them reinforcing (e.g., edibles).

B. Secondary or conditioned reinforcers: these you have learned to like via pairing with more naturally-reinforcing consequences (e.g., praise or "gold stars").

C. Generalized reinforcers: these are reinforcers that can be traded in for other reinforcers as might be seen in a token economy, for example.

D. Premack or activity reinforcers: the opportunity to engage in high probability behaviors (those the student is more likely to engage in, probably more preferred activities) is used to reinforce a lower probability behavior (ones the student is not as likely to engage in without an incentive).

68. What if a student cannot or will not give up a reinforcer once it is earned?

If a child cannot easily give up a given reinforcer (e.g., a particular toy), that reinforcer may not always be usable. We are hesitant to give up motivating reinforcers, however. More frequently, therefore, we continue to attempt to use the reinforcer. While the student may tantrum initially when the reinforcer is taken back, as (s)he learns that the reinforcer comes and goes, and that it will return nearly immediately upon compliance with requests, the student will learn to more easily give up the reinforcer. Specific programming may be needed to teach the skill of giving up the toy and getting it back. For example, it may be necessary to deliver a different, special reinforcer just for giving up the original reinforcer. Another strategy might be to initially return the toy to the student immediately, and only gradually build in a delay and added demands before giving the reinforcer back.

69. Should we use continuous or intermittent reinforcement?

That depends on what you are trying to accomplish. Both continuous and intermittent schedules of reinforcement have their place in programming. Continuous reinforcement means that every time the target behavior is emitted, it is reinforced. To use some technical vocabulary, we could call this a Fixed Ratio 1 schedule. Continuous reinforcement is very important when we are first introducing skills. It gives immediate and constant feedback to shape behavior. It creates new behavior rapidly and maintains behavior as long as it is in effect. It is rarely used in the long-term, however, as behavior under this schedule has little resistance to extinction. In other words, behavior that has been maintained by continuous reinforcement extinguishes (goes away) relatively quickly once the behavior is no longer being reinforced. Consider a student who has learned to make requests through continuous reinforcement. If the student suddenly entered a real world setting where people were not able to immediately grant requests, the response might extinguish very rapidly (and might even be accompanied by an ugly extinction burst).

In contrast, intermittent reinforcement refers to reinforcing only some instances of a given behavior, not every time the behavior is emitted. In contrast to continuous reinforcement, intermittent reinforcement generally leads to behavior that is more resistant to extinction (i.e., the difference between how much money people put into slot machines versus broken soda machines).

So, should one use continuous or intermittent reinforcement? Again, it depends on the goal. When teaching a new skill, one would likely use continuous reinforcement. In order to guard against extinction of the skill, however, we would gradually fade towards more intermittent reinforcement.

As a final note on the issue, NEVER intermittently reinforce behavior that you wish to see decrease. While it is paradoxical to say, carrying out a treatment plan correctly more often than not can be worse than never beginning the plan. Consider what would happen if one reinforced a student's head-banging by allowing the child to avoid a task when (s)he head-banged. Now think about what would happen if you only allowed the child to avoid every once in a while though head-banging. How does the student know when head-banging will "pay off" and when it will not? (S)he doesn't, and therefore tends to engage in the behavior for a much longer time than if the behavior had been continuously reinforced and then extinguished. This effect is often accompanied by the behavior-altering properties of the extinction burst (see Chapter XVI, Questions #100 and #101), and it is a potentially lethal combination. Don't begin a behavior treatment plan unless you're ready to carry it through the whole way.

70. How do we find reinforcers?

There is an enormous array of items and activities in this world that are potential reinforcers. Some learners find many of these things to be reinforcing. Other learners have a more restricted range of current reinforcers.

One of the best ways of finding reinforcers is by simply asking people who know the learner well. Obtaining a list of specific information about favorite items and activities can be a huge time saver. Make sure to gather very specific information about the preferred items and activities, as preferences are often very specific. For example, a learner who finds it highly reinforcing to manipulate green clay may not find other brands or colors of similar stuff to be so cool.

It is also important to remember that the value of reinforcers often changes over time. Edibles do not hold the same value after the learner has just eaten a hearty lunch (an effect called *satiation*). Items that are contacted frequently may become less valuable than those that have not been contacted in a while (and therefore we sometimes need to use *deprivation* wherein we limit access to specific items to increase their reinforcer value).

The bottom line is that we must continually consider the value of items and activities in order to make sure that they are functioning as reinforcers. If the student possesses sufficient communication skills, we can simply ask the learner what they want "to work for." Other times, we do a more formal reinforcer assessment, wherein we systematically present two items simultaneously to see which item the learner will select. By repeatedly making such pairwise comparisons, we can create a hierarchy of reinforcer value. For learners with few identified reinforcers or when items do not appear to be working as reinforcers, such formalized reinforcer assessment must be conducted. Always keep in mind, however, that reinforcer value can change from moment to moment and therefore we need to stay alert and monitor the student's ongoing motivation for the item.

71. How do we teach new reinforcers?

A few simple procedures can be used to establish new reinforcers. For many students, certain stimuli are not reinforcing simply because the students have not been exposed to them, either through lack of opportunity or reluctance to try new things. As my (DR) mother always said about new foods, "Try it, you might like it!" Often, simply exposing students to new activities and foods is sufficient to increase reinforcer value of these items. This is called *reinforcer sampling*, and is achieved by allowing non-contingent access to items. The student who may not be willing to work for an unknown activity or food may be willing to try it if (s)he does not have to put forth effort to get it. Once sampled, the item might take on reinforcing properties and become a motivator for other behavior.

If the student is unwilling to try something new, a reinforcement contingency can be put into place whereby an established reinforcer can be offered for sampling the new activity or food. For example, a student might be given small pieces of his favorite potato chips as he plays with a new toy. This has the dual benefit of reinforcing the desired behavior of engaging in a new activity while *pairing* the new activity with an established reinforcer. This pairing process is the basic procedure for creating conditioned reinforcers, basically resulting in the association of a neutral or unknown stimulus with a known pleasurable one. Ultimately, the new stimulus takes on the pleasurable associations of the established reinforcer.

72. Should we use edible reinforcers?

Edibles can serve as excellent reinforcers for many learners, particularly when they have not yet learned to appreciate other reinforcers. Just remember that as the learner receives more and more edibles at a given time, satiation may occur and the value of the edibles may decrease. Also remember simple rules of physiology. The value of a salty food may decrease if a beverage is not also occasionally offered to the learner.

Over the course of time, we want to fade towards more normalized, everyday reinforcers such as praise and favored activities. Therefore, we always pair edibles with praise and other more naturally occurring reinforcers. In this way, the more naturally occurring reinforcers become *conditioned reinforcers* and we can start to fade back on edibles.

As an example, suppose that we institute a token economy (see below). The student can earn tokens during an activity, and trade them in for a larger edible reinforcer at the end of the period (e.g., a cup or small package of the edibles). This is roughly equivalent to what we do when we tell ourselves, "I'll go get a snack from the vending machine AS SOON AS I finish this..."(even if we don't always mark our own progress with tokens). Of course, we will supply a menu of reinforcers for the student to choose from, which will include edibles as well as activities, toys, etc.

73. What is a token economy?

A token economy is a system wherein individuals earn arbitrarily chosen, initially neutral, stimuli, and these stimuli are used as generalized reinforcers as part of a behavior management or teaching system. In other words, token economies are a system of exchange wherein students can earn tokens through their behavior, and these tokens are then exchanged for other commodities or activities. This is quite normalizing (consider the paychecks that we all earn for working and then trade in for other commodities). Token economies also stretch out the supply of other reinforcers (e.g., you may have to earn five tokens to trade in for an edible reinforcer). Tokens also guard against satiation. Whoever satiates on (has enough) money? Similarly, students working with token economies do not satiate on tokens if you use the system properly (i.e., having lots of cool stuff to trade in for).

Please remember that a token economy will only be as good as the items/activities that the tokens can buy. It is useless to have a really well-designed token economy, but nothing the student finds reinforcing to buy with the tokens (s)he has earned. Make sure you have a potent reinforcer menu!

74. How do we start a token economy?

To begin a token economy, choose the commodity you are going to use as the medium of exchange. Poker chips, coins, stickers, decorated pieces of laminated cardboard, and points on a point board are common choices.

Once you decide on the commodity, begin to introduce the system to the student. Have a good supply of the reinforcers (s)he has already been earning and that you are sure function as reinforcers. Give the student a token without asking the student to perform any skill (noncontingently) and immediately ask for it back. As soon as you have the token back, provide the older, established reinforcer. Do this a number of times. When the student begins to give you the token without prompting, you're ready for the next step.

Once the student is giving you back the token and anticipating the exchange, introduce a response requirement. Ask the student to demonstrate a skill that is easy for the student (e.g., touching his head). Reinforce the performance of this skill by giving a token and then immediately requesting it back. In other words, you are making the exchange just as you had when you were providing tokens noncontingently. You have just awarded the student's first contingent token. Do this several times to establish the new contingency.

Of course, you really haven't stretched out the supply of reinforcers yet. The student is still getting one of the old reinforcers after every successful trial. Now is the time to stretch things out. Again, have the student perform the skill that had been acquired to fluency, for example touching his head, just as you did before. Give the token. When the student looks to trade in the token, quickly prompt the student to demonstrate the skill again. When the student performs the skill, give another token. The student will now trade in the *two* tokens for the older reinforcer. Repeat this procedure to begin gradually increasing the number of tokens the student must earn to trade in. Create a menu with different prices for different reinforcers. Don't build up behavioral or token exchange requirements too quickly or the behavior may extinguish. You'll be looking for too much effort ("too expensive") for the reinforcer too soon.

75. Should we use a token economy?

Token economies are a great tool for increasing the delay before obtaining access to a preferred item or activity. It gives the learner a visual cue to remind him or her that backup reinforcement is getting closer. Token economies can also be used on a variable ratio or variable interval schedule. For example, the learner may be able to earn a token for every 3 to 5 responses instead of just setting a specific number of responses that are needed. This builds in the advantages of using variable schedules of reinforcement (e.g., it could be the next one).

When using token economies, the token itself is paired with backup reinforcers and the actual delivery of the token becomes reinforcing. This is highly normalizing, as we all participate in a great big token economy (the monetary system). Learners can also be taught to independently use token economies as a way of self-monitoring their behavior.

76. What's up with that descriptive praise thing?

The stereotype of the behavior analyst (sometimes called "behavior geek," although we prefer the term "action nerd") is of someone giving out rather odd-sounding praise: "good sitting!," "good looking," or "good following directions!"

We use this descriptive (sometimes called "telegraphic") praise during the earlier stages of programming. Remember that many students diagnosed with autistic-spectrum disorders demonstrate deficits in social understanding. If you say "great job," the student may not realize what you mean. You meant to praise a nice social initiation, but the person thought you were praising good posture and feet on the floor. We attempt to avoid such misunderstandings through the use of descriptive praise.

It is important to note that we fade such praise as the student gets ready for more mainstream settings. This just isn't the way people talk in "real life," except in behavior analysts' homes. There you can hear "nice passing the remote, honey" on a regular basis between spouses.

77. Should we use contingent or noncontingent reinforcement?

Providing noncontingent reinforcement means that there is no relationship between the learner's behavior and the reinforcers that are given. In general, noncontingent reinforcement should only be used in special circumstances, such as in a behavior plan designed to break the relationship between a behavior and a consequence.

Noncontingent reinforcement is also often used at the beginning of learner-teacher relationships. This helps the teacher to become a conditioned reinforcer him/herself, and also lets the student experience what sorts of reinforcers are available ("reinforcer sampling").

As a rule of thumb, learners acquire skills better when reinforcement is contingent upon their performance. Even when reinforcers are delivered to learners freely during pairing procedures, however, the delivery of reinforcers should never coincide with, or immediately follow, challenging behavior.

Chapter XIV

Fine-tuning for Programming and

Advanced Considerations

78. When/how should we work towards generalization?

To program for stimulus generalization, one systematically varies non-essential aspects of the teaching environment ("loose teaching"). As we have jokingly characterized the procedure, it is the "Dr. Seuss" approach: practice the skill "in a house and with a mouse, in a box and with a fox." But seriously, make sure that you:

- A. Have a number of individuals providing instruction.
- B. Have several sets of stimuli for teaching purposes.
- C. Use varied phrasing of instructions.
- D. Practice in different settings.
- E. Practice at different times of day.
- F. Etc.

There are differing schools of thought regarding when to begin working towards generalization. Some interventionists prefer to teach a given skill "to criteria," using an extremely limited set of stimuli and instructions. Once the student has achieved the mastery criterion, one then begins to generalize the skill, step by step. Variations are introduced slowly and systematically, again building to criterion before moving to the next variation.

Other interventionists prefer to work towards generalization from the beginning. From the first day of introducing a new skill, they use multiple sets of stimuli and instructional phrasings. The idea is to prevent failure to generalize by building generalization into the teaching procedure from the beginning. While acquisition will probably be slower under these circumstances, avoiding a tendency to "dig a hole that you have to climb out of" will make long-term generalization much easier. We tend to go along with this latter conception, contingent upon student performance. Of course, we can never forget that ABA is a data-based discipline. If the data indicate that a student is unable to make expected gains with the "generalization from the beginning" strategy, one can teach using fewer exemplars and instructions and settings and then gradually build them in.

79. What should we use as a mastery criterion?

Once again, we will say it in unison - "it depends." Different skills have to be performed at different levels of "mastery" in order to be functional. Would you fly with an airline that made a proper landing 9 out of 10 times? On the other hand, the best hitters in professional baseball only get a hit three or four times out of ten. When the nice police officer says "Let me see your license," (s)he will not simply repeat the request if you do not respond. You probably also won't find the physical prompt for the correct response to the request to be reinforcing. And, from personal experience, we can also assure you that responding "I'll give you my license if you let me play with your flashlight" is *not* a response that is likely to be reinforced. Such flippancy aside, there is also the matter of latency to respond. You have to comply with the instruction within a given time period for it to be reinforced. You get the idea.

Therefore, we suggest setting a *general* mastery criterion, but then altering it based upon the needs inherent in the task. Consider the following general criterion: "90% accuracy, across three consecutive sessions, across at least two interventionists." This forms a starting point. You have achieved a given level of success, a given level of stability, and at least some degree of generalization across instructors (please note, however, our discussion regarding isolated versus randomized material and the mastery criterion issues contained therein).

For many tasks, the best way to set mastery criterion is to ascertain the average performance of typically-developing peers for the same behavior. Consider the issue of "on-task" behavior. If you were going to set the mastery criterion for a fourth grade student to be on-task within class, what would it be? By looking at the peer group, you would have a social norm reference to guide you (and you might be surprised at what the range of typical peer group performance actually is). We suggest plotting a "band" of typical behavior levels on the graph, and then aiming for the performance of your student to fit within that typical band.

As a final note on this matter, remember that more is not always better. Manding 400 times in 30 minutes is hardly typical and would serve to socially ostracize the student (and can become quite annoying). Even "appropriate" behavior can be displayed too frequently. Consider the student who is sitting quietly, with hands neatly folded, while everyone else is behaving in a silly manner at the school cafeteria. That student is not engaging in appropriate behavior *for that setting* and is likely missing out on some great socialization opportunities. That student has to learn to run amok with everyone else, when the time is right for it.

80. How do we choose outside mainstreaming and recreation activities?

Mainstreaming activities are those activities that the student diagnosed with autism will engage in along with typically-developing peers. There are several key issues to consider when deciding on mainstreaming activities. First and foremost, we want the activity to foster interaction with typically-developing peers. Activities will vary in the degree to which they foster communication and social interaction. Swimming, for example, is a common choice. It is not always the best one, however. As George Carlin once remarked, "swimming is a way to keep from drowning." Unless specific play and social activities have been planned for the water, it is not often a highly social or communicative activity. Art activities where students must share materials, or play activities where students interact together over the toys or athletic equipment are probably better choices.

Second, we must consider what skills the student has developed to this point. We want the mainstreaming experience to be meaningful, and for the student to actually participate in activities with peers. Simply being in the same room is rarely sufficient, unless we are working on a goal of tolerating peer proximity, or perhaps desensitizing to the ambient noise of a group of children. During our intensive teaching, we would do well to pre-practice the skills that the student will need in the mainstreaming setting. This involves planning, and generally observing the setting where the student will mainstream, well in advance. With this advanced "intelligence," we know what skills will be necessary for the student to possess (e.g., getting on line at school, taking turns shooting baskets, catching and throwing, sharing crayons, etc.).

Third, how structured is the activity? Many programmers in schools choose to start mainstreaming in "specials" such as music, art, physical education, and lunch. This may be appropriate for some students, but can be difficult for others. Remember that in early stages of ABA programming, students often become accustomed to a highly structured and often relatively quiet setting. Students with autism differ in their ability to adjust from such a highly structured setting to a classroom environment. The individual strengths and needs of the given student must be considered when planning mainstreaming. A student who is sensitive to noise, for example, would not do well in a music class. Similarly, the skills and teaching style of the teachers in the mainstreaming setting should be considered. A student with autism might show facility with art skills, but not do well in a mainstream art class that is conducted very loosely by a teacher who does not provide a lot of direction. On the other hand, the physical education teacher might run a highly-structured class that would be perfect for a particular student.

Remember that you should pick and choose activities wisely, and stack the deck for success. We generally suggest beginning mainstreaming in "mock" situations, with peers who have been coached as to how to behave with the student diagnosed with autism, and how to be reinforcing (e.g., Odom & Strain 1986).

From there, we can begin fading towards more naturally occurring situations.

81. When should we begin mainstreaming?

Generally speaking, begin mainstreaming as soon as two conditions are satisfied:

> A. The student has developed the skills to meaningfully take part in the activity.
>
> B. Behavior that is competing with learning or which will draw inappropriate attention to the student are under control.

We want this to be a reinforcing activity for the student, and to begin pairing other children with reinforcement. That will not happen if (s)he cannot interact with peers, or participate in any activities. It will certainly not happen if the other children are making fun of the student due to aberrant behavior.

82. So what's the difference between mainstreaming and inclusion?

The answer to this question will depend on who you ask. Unfortunately, while the words have technical meanings, many people use the terms interchangeably in everyday discourse.

Generally speaking, the difference has to do with the amount of support and environmental modifications required for the student to participate in certain environments. Advocates of mainstreaming usually suggest that the student diagnosed with an ASD should go into classes with typically-developing peers for only carefully selected parts of the day. Inclusion advocates push for full-day participation with typically developing peers. Both provide for necessary supports, but the inclusion model generally requires far more support and modification within the target environment than the mainstreaming model does.

Leaving the vocabulary aside, we believe the important questions facing parents and teachers/clinicians are relatively straightforward:

    A.   Does the student possess sufficient skills to be able to benefit from the placement? If so, for all areas or just for some?

    B.   Related to the previous questions, how much time will the student spend in settings with typically developing peers? Will it be all day, or only carefully chosen activities?

    C.   How much support will be needed to make this experience successful socially and educationally? Is this support available, or can it be made available?

    D.   How shall we fade supports as the student develops the necessary skills?

The key point here is that any student *can* be placed into a class of typically developing peers. That does not ensure, however, that the experience will be in any way meaningful for the student. The placement setting may not provide instruction in a manner that is conducive to the student's learning abilities and prerequisite skills. In other words, we don't want the student simply sitting in the classroom if (s)he is not optimally learning there, or placed into overstimulating environments such as the cafeteria if (s)he has not yet developed the skills to tolerate that level of stimulation.

While we are huge fans of having the student interact with typically-developing peers, we are also fans of ensuring that the necessary skills have previously been developed, and that the necessary supports are in place. The alternative, which is all too common, is that the student diagnosed with an ASD winds up sitting in the back of the room, accompanied by his/her aide. The student functions as a satellite that moves around the room and the rest of the children, but never truly interacts. The school years tick away, without the student developing the skills that will be necessary in future life. Somewhere during this process, it is often noted that the student in question is several years behind the rest of the class in academic, social and language skills. The student is then blamed for this, as though it was somehow his/her fault, as opposed to the more proper attribution of failing to plan instruction and support properly (see also our early commentary regarding Positive Behavioral Support).

Chapter XV
Discrete Trial Teaching

83. What is discrete trial teaching?

Discrete-trial teaching (DTT) is the Antecedent → Behavior → Consequence paradigm applied to teaching new skills. It is an extremely effective teaching method for children with autism. Through the use of repeated, succinct instructions and stimuli, followed by corrective procedures or positive reinforcement, children can learn important, functional skills. Families may find dramatic improvements in their lives as their children learn to communicate appropriately, play, follow instructions, and take care of their own personal needs. Like any technical procedure, however, DTT is often misused and misunderstood.

The first myth to dispel is that DTT is sufficient intervention unto itself. DTT is useful for teaching new skills, but is not sufficient for generalization of these skills to the natural environment. Nor should it continue to be used when it is no longer needed. A common mistake is in keeping children in unnecessarily restrictive programs after they are learning from their natural environment. Furthermore, DTT is only effective as long as it is followed through in the natural environment. Parents and teachers cannot expect lasting behavior change or long-term improvements by providing a certain number of hours of DTT per week, and then failing to ensure that students are practicing the skills that they are learning in their "real lives."

In DTT, an instruction or other stimulus is presented by the teacher. If the student follows this with a correct response, some form of positive reinforcement is presented. If the student does not respond or responds incorrectly, some form of correction is presented, usually a prompt for the correct response. Each presentation of a stimulus and the resulting behavior and consequence is a trial; trials are presented repeatedly. The teacher records the student's responses on each trial, and these data are used to analyze the effectiveness of the teaching procedure and to decide when to increase task demands or difficulty.

The procedure looks easy to use and can be easy to teach people to use. Problems arise when it is used in a rigid format, with no regard for the individual learning style of the student. Because of a lack of skilled experts in many areas, families often choose to recruit college students or family members, and then train them to provide DTT. While this is a good strategy for obtaining cost-effective treatment, it must be heavily supervised by a very competent and experienced behavior analyst. The behavior of the teacher in DTT is often scripted and controlled for consistency; the problems arise when teachers cannot leave the script to make use of teachable moments that have not been anticipated.

DTT is often misunderstood and applied incorrectly. When used inappropriately, poor DTT can lead to increased behavior problems, robotic responding, and failure to generalize. There are steep costs to using this procedure incorrectly, including an overall social movement to reduce its use. This could lead to many children not receiving an appropriate and helpful method of teaching.

84. What should be taught in drills and what should be taught incidentally?

This is not an easily answered question. Generally speaking, a common maxim is to avoid drilling anything that is being learned incidentally. Consider, for example, the section on teaching eye contact. A student may learn the skill through simple shaping. When this learning is not occurring, however, drilling can be conducted. Even in this context, however, we recommend combining the eye contact with other drills so as to more closely approximate normal interactions (again, unless data suggest that this strategy is not being effective). You would take the eye contact data sheet out of the book, for example, and simultaneously keep data on the eye contact and whatever skill you have paired it with. Remember to maintain eye contact requirements even when not collecting data, however.

To take another common example, consider the "social greetings" drill. This can be done, sitting at a table and repeatedly practicing the verbal exchange. While this might be needed for some students, it also removes the verbal interaction from its natural context. Perhaps the same "drill" could be conducted as frequently, but interspersed throughout the day. Each time the student or staff member leaves the room and returns is an opportunity to "conduct a trial," as opposed to repeatedly performing the drill despite the fact that neither student nor interventionist has moved anywhere. Do you repeat greetings like that in everyday interactions? If not, it is probably best to avoid such drilling unless data show that it is necessary for the student. If interspersing trials throughout the day, remember to follow the same data collection, reinforcement, and error correction procedures as you would do if you were sitting down to provide instruction as a drill.

85. Must we do discrete trial teaching face-to- face, knee-to-knee?

Students will unquestionably attend better to instructions if they are seated properly, and not otherwise engaged in problem behavior or stereotypy. Teaching only under these circumstances pretty much ensures that students will not learn to attend in real-life situations, however. If the student is expected to attend to a teacher's instructions in a large group, for example, there won't be anyone there making sure that they are seated perfectly. In the real world, children often have to hear instructions that are given while they are playing, walking, or even running. DTT can and should take place anywhere – sometimes at the table, sometimes in the yard or on the bed or the floor. Newer, more difficult skills can be taught under more controlled conditions, but teaching and practice should be taken into the natural environment as quickly as possible. Wherever you are providing instruction, remember to keep to your structured framework and maintain the data-collection procedures that will allow you to determine the effectiveness of the intervention.

86. Must teaching follow a pre-set curriculum?

A well-designed curriculum allows teachers to make systematic choices regarding what to teach students, and to ensure that students are learning age-appropriate skills. A pre-written curriculum does not address the student's individual needs in his or her real environment, however. Learning to dress one's self might be a bigger priority for a family than learning to write. If the curriculum demands that writing come first, however, the child will not learn the more important skill in his life as early as possible. One occupational therapist that I (DR) worked with insisted that our mutual student was not writing the letter "M" with me because he had not yet demonstrated the ability to draw a square. When I showed her the page of Ms he had made earlier that day, she told me that the were not in fact Ms . . . but M-shaped lines. This is the product of adherence to a curriculum. Worse, another student of mine was prevented from using the picture-exchange communication system that she had successfully been using to make requests for several months. In her new school, children were not given access to this augmentative communication system until they had met a series of criteria for mastery of matching skills. These examples highlight the importance of using the curriculum only as a guide and not a pre-set sequence of goals. Prioritization and appropriate sequencing of goals is an ongoing process.

Sometimes children are held back from learning useful, functional skills because they have not yet mastered earlier curriculum items. Instead, the curriculum should be used as a guide. A well-trained programmer should be able, along with the student's parents, to evaluate the most crucial needs for that student and to address those needs first.

87. Must we accept only the response written in the program book?

This is another rule based upon the importance of consistency. If one person expects a student to answer in full sentences, and no one else does, that creates confusion and frustration all around. Specifying the response that is expected of the student is a good idea, being sure to encourage varied appropriate phrasings. After all, if a student says "You can call me Al," isn't that just as good as saying "My name is Al"? Variation in responding should always be reinforced for students diagnosed with autism, who often have difficulty with response variation. The common misconception that DTT necessarily leads to robotic responding comes from this type of error. Programs would better specify a rule (e.g., a sentence of at least three words that gives the important information) for the correct response, or give several examples of correct responses, rather than the specified words of the response.

88. Must all teachers use the same prompts?

In the interest of consistency, DTT program are frequently written to include prompting procedures. This level of detail is often necessary, but not always. Often, a given skill can be taught fully and prompts faded within a session. Excessively planning prompts can lead to their overuse, and thus prompt-dependency. Ideally, teachers should be sufficiently well-trained to be able to plan and fade prompts within a short period of time. Prompts and the fading of prompts should be based upon data collected.

89. Must we use the same reinforcer for a given program all the time?

Just as prompts are often planned for the sake of consistency, so are reinforcers. This is not always necessary, and can be detrimental to the program. Using the same reinforcers all the time makes them less effective (satiation), and forgets that students' preferences can change from day to day or even hour to hour. Better to have the student choose his or her reinforcers frequently throughout a teaching session, and change reinforcers often so that students don't become habituated to the reinforcers.

90. Is it true that nothing is more important than the Data and the Book?

Teachers and programmers love their data books. These tattered, overstuffed binders are guarded fiercely. Parents also develop some affection for them. But sometimes you have to chuck the book and just play with and teach the student. It is unquestionably necessary to have written programs and clear, accurate data to guide decision-making. It is also necessary, however, to have teachers (and parents) who are able to capture teachable moments that are not specified in the program book.

91. Can we work on skills other than those that are in the program book?

Given that teachers in DTT programs are often (and unfortunately!!!!) minimally trained, program coordinators often prefer to limit teacher activities to the prescribed and scripted programs in the data collection book that is the ubiquitous center of these programs. While it's best for an untrained person to avoid potential problems by sticking with what they've been shown how to do, if someone is really that untrained, they probably shouldn't be working with a child without supervision. The point is, children do great things all the time. Every moment is a teachable moment. Teachers should not be considered to be trained until they are able to recognize, reinforce, and work from naturally occurring behavior that the child may offer outside of the programs in "the book."

92. Is it true that once a student acquires a skill in discrete trial teaching that the job is done?

Most DTT programs specify a criterion for when a skill is considered to be mastered. That criterion is usually expressed as some number of correct responses per opportunities. While it is important to have an objective criterion for mastery, it is not sufficient to teach a skill to mastery in a segregated setting. Rather, teachers must ensure that the student can display the skill in a variety of contexts, with different people and different materials, and in the absence of obvious external reinforcement. Skills are not truly mastered until they are being displayed functionally in the real world. To promote generalization, mastery should be assessed across settings, stimuli, and instructors. We recommend building this into the mastery criterion itself (e.g., 90% correct responding across 3 days and 2 interventionists).

93. Should we keep up high intensity discrete trial teaching for as long as possible?

DTT is very effective, and it is often the first procedure that really leads to significant changes for children with autism. Parents and teachers are therefore often hesitant to stop doing it. After all, if it isn't broken, don't fix it. It is, however, important to fade DTT when possible. Every effort should be made to have learning occur under circumstances that are as normal as possible, so that the child can function in the real world. Functional, real-life skills should be taught, and teaching should be the least restrictive possible. As soon a student begins to learn from his or her environment, DTT should be limited to lagging areas.

94. Isn't discrete trial teaching boring and aversive?

DTT does not need to boring, restrictive, or unpleasant for the child. A well-trained teacher can make it fun, functional, and an active process for the student as well as the teacher. In addition to the above suggestions, incorporating a lot of choice opportunities for the student can help. Allowing the student to choose reinforcers, materials, and even programs to work on can dramatically limit competing behavior during teaching (Newman, Needelman, Reinecke, & Robek, 2002). Additionally, teachers need to be well-trained. It is not sufficient to learn a set of procedures; teachers must have a good working knowledge of the principles and literature of applied behavior analysis in order to be flexible and effective teachers.

Chapter XVI

Behavior Management

95. What is the difference between functional *assessment* and functional *analysis*?

Both functional analysis and functional assessment are methods to help us uncover and understand the variables maintaining a given behavior. Despite the similarity in name, there is a notable difference between the two. The key difference is the degree to which the environment is manipulated by the investigator. With functional assessment, we seek to answer the question of *what* is causing a given behavior by carefully observing the behavior occurring in the settings where it has been previously observed. In functional analysis, the environment is manipulated to create a mini-experiment. We contrive conditions and deliberately manipulate variables (e.g., creating a high demand condition where the behavior in question would allow escape, then creating a low demand condition where the behavior would allow escape, then creating a high demand condition where the behavior would not allow escape, etc.). Functional analysis is sometimes conducted in the setting where the behavior is naturally occurring, but it is usually conducted in a different location in order to control for all other variables. Functional assessment, however, is always conducted in the setting where the behavior is occurring. In either case, the antecedents, behavior and consequences of that behavior are carefully observed so as to determine possible functions for the behavior in question.

There are benefits and drawbacks to each procedure. Obviously, functional analysis allows for a greater degree of control over the situation. It is possible, however, to entirely miss the real reason the behavior was being displayed when conditions are contrived. Even if a functional analysis is conducted in the setting where the behavior is occurring, you may miss the naturally occurring reason while you are manipulating variables (e.g., the tantrums were actually due to another student covertly kicking under the table all along, and no one had observed this).

In general, we suggest beginning with functional assessment, and then moving into a more contrived functional analysis if the controlling variables are not identified.

96. How do we choose behavior management strategies?

This falls in the area of functional analysis and functional assessment. As we have often remarked, anyone who wants to tell you that they can give you a treatment plan without first conducting a functional analysis or assessment of the behavior in question is selling something. Functional analysis and assessment involves investigating the variables that will allow us to determine the answer to the key question, "why is he DOING that?" Note that the question is *not* "why did he start?" Sometimes behavior can start for one reason, but then continue on for other reasons ("take on a life of its own"). Being more scientific about it, the question would be phrased, "what are the variables maintaining behavior now?" The general steps are as follows:

108

Step 1

Define the behavior in such a way that everyone interacting with the student can agree when it has happened and when it has not.

Step 2

Establish an appropriate data-collection strategy for the behavior in question (e.g., frequency, rate, percentage, latency, magnitude, duration, etc.).

Step 3

BASELINE: observe the behavior under a variety of conditions to assess its level for comparison purposes and collect A--> B --> C data (Antecedent --> Behavior --> Consequence).

Step 4

Draft a hypothesis regarding the function of the behavior, based upon what is observed during baseline, particularly the A --> B --> C observations.

Step 5

Test your hypothesis by carrying out the treatment plan logically suggested by your analysis of the A--> B --> C observations. If the plan does not work, if behavior is not moving in the desired direction, reassess. Did you carry out the plan improperly, or is it the wrong plan? Go back to step three.

Note that the same behavior can occur for diametrically opposite reasons. This would then call for diametrically opposed treatment plans. To cite the example we provided in *Behaviorspeak* (2003), if one believes that a given self-injurious behavior serves an attention-seeking function, one would not approach an individual who is engaging in the SIB. In contrast, if the student instead engages in this behavior for avoidance reasons, one would not terminate the interaction with the student while the behavior was occurring. The key issue to remember is that we are always in the realm of experiment, manipulating variables in order to assess the effect on behavior. As Sherlock Holmes summarized in *A Scandal in Bohemia:* it is a capital mistake to formulate theories before one has all the available facts. One winds up twisting new facts to meet old theories, rather than old theories to meet new facts.

97. What do we do if the behavior has more than one function?

More often than we would like, our assessment to determine the function of a problem behavior indicates that there are multiple functions for the behavior. For example, a functional assessment could reveal that a student shows a pattern of engaging in inappropriate vocalizations following a demand (functioning as escape), as well as when staff members are working with another child (functioning as attention-seeking). As with any behavior plan, the treatment plan logically suggested by the analysis is implemented for a behavior with more than one function. In the previous example, the treatment plan would include more than one possible consequence to the problem behavior, depending on the antecendent (what occurred just before the behavior). If the inappropriate vocalization occurred after the student was given an instruction, the demand would not be lifted until the student completed the instruction without engaging in the problem behavior. If the inappropriate vocalization occurred when the staff member turned around to assist another student, the plan might include ignoring the behavior. Additional treatment components are often added in order to differentially reinforce other behavior (DRO) or differentially reinforce incompatible behavior (DRI). In some cases, a punishment procedure (e.g., response cost or time out from reinforcement) is incorporated into the behavior plan. When one of the functions associated with the problem behavior is related to a skill deficit (e.g., tolerating a delay before accessing preferred activities), additional programs may be implemented to target that skill area.

As with any behavior plan, it is crucial that ongoing data collection (using the appropriate data-collection strategy for the behavior) is conducted. If data analysis indicates that the behavior is not moving in the desired direction, the plan should be reassessed. Remember that a behavior plan that includes extinction procedures may result in a temporary extinction burst. If it is not possible to continue the extinction procedure to completion due to the behavior becoming dangerous, a behavior plan including extinction should not be implemented.

98. How do we state behavior goals?

Behavior goals are stated very precisely. There are three components that should be part of any good behavior goal. These include:

    A. What behavior should be performed.

    B. Under what circumstances the behavior should be performed.

C. A quantitative measure of the behavior (e.g., rate, duration, etc.).

The way we often state a behavior goal should specify what behavior should occur, under what circumstances, and how much of it. Notice a poorly written goal: "I will try to get to the gym more." Note that there are no specifics. We could watch the person for a full year and not know if they are "trying to get to the gym more." But if the goal is written more precisely, such as "will ride the exercise bike at 70% of aerobic capacity at the gym on Monday, Wednesday and Friday nights, for 20 minutes," now there is no ambiguity. We would know if the goal is being met or not.

99. What is the Dead Man's (Person's) Test?

The Dead Man's (Person's) Test is a guideline used when creating behavior treatment plans and behavior goals in general. The basic idea is that anything a dead person can do is not behavior and therefore shouldn't be a part of a treatment plan. In other words, if the dead could satisfy behavioral requirements, then it is not a good plan. Dead people, for example, do not run around the room (as far as we know). Therefore "not running around the room" fails the dead man's test.

This guideline reminds us that we need to concentrate on the behavior that we want to see, not the behavior that we don't want to see. Our general goal is to increase desired behavior, which leaves less time for engaging in inappropriate behavior, and possibly decreases motivation to engage in the inappropriate behavior. Consider the common goal of toilet training. This generally begins by teaching the individual how and when to eliminate. If your plan mistakenly emphasizes not having accidents, all you have done is teach the individual to hold it in (and now you wonder why they're getting larger). The bottom line is that we cannot expect that just by decreasing an inappropriate behavior that a person will spontaneously develop a more appropriate one in its stead. In fact, the opposite is often the case – if a more appropriate alternative is not taught, the person may begin to engage in another undesirable behavior to replace the old one.

100. What is the difference between ignoring and extinction?

The answer to this question goes back to the basic definition of "extinction." Remember that an extinction plan means that a behavior is not reinforced. That is not the same as showing no reaction (ignoring). An extinction plan may or may not involve ignoring the behavior. As long as a reinforcer is not forthcoming for a given behavior, you are conducting an extinction plan.

Consider a person who is spitting as an avoidance behavior. The person is seeking to avoid an interaction and spits on you. Is it a proper extinction plan if you wipe off the spit? Of course it is, as long as you continue the interaction. You are not providing the reinforcer of terminating the interaction, even though you did not ignore the behavior, and thus you are still conducting an extinction plan. As always, remember that you need to know what the reinforcer actually is before you can institute an effective extinction plan.

101. What is an extinction burst?

The *extinction burst* refers to the tendency for behavior to get worse before it gets better when a previously reinforced behavior is no longer reinforced.   We call it a burst when the behavior *temporarily* increases in frequency, magnitude, and variability following the institution of the extinction plan.

The crucial warning must always be made when discussing extinction plans: if it is not possible to continue the extinction procedure to completion due to variations in behavior becoming dangerous or intolerable, then one *should not begin* the extinction plan. Otherwise, one might inadvertently make the behavior worse than it had been previously.

102. Should inappropriate behavior be ignored?

This brings us back to our question that opened this section regarding how behavior management strategies should be selected. The key point that we must always return to is the function of the behavior.   Should an inappropriate behavior be ignored? Remember our two words that begin nearly every answer in Applied Behavior Analysis: "it depends." Is the inappropriate behavior in question being performed for attention-seeking or reaction-seeking reasons? If so, then an ignoring strategy may be the appropriate one.

That being said, the fact that the textbooks would tell you to ignore an inappropriate behavior does not mean that you can always practically do so. To take one example from my (BN) own clinical background, a girl at one of our school programs would run from the classroom several times a day. A careful functional analysis told us what everyone had suspected all along: the behavior had a large attention-seeking component. She found the chase reinforcing. The dual strategies the research and clinical literature suggested were:

A. Increase reinforcement available in the classroom.

B. Do not chase, because doing so will accidentally reinforce the behavior.

This being said, it was impossible to carry out the second portion of the treatment plan. The girl simply had no conception of the danger posed by speeding cars. She had run away from her parents onto a busy highway one weekend. Our school was located near a very busy road. If we would have attempted to ignore the behavior when the girl was running towards an outside door and there was no adult between her and the street, the outcome might have been tragic. We had no choice. Physical safety must be a paramount concern in all behavior management decisions. Parents and staff often find themselves confronted with such decisions when considering behavior such as self-injury, climbing, handling sharp objects, or running from others. The good news is that behavior plans can be carefully designed to effectively reduce the problem behavior and maintain the safety of the child.

103. What is the difference between systematic desensitization and flooding?

Systematic desensitization and flooding are both methods for reducing fears or over-sensitivity to stimuli through the process of exposure. They differ markedly in how they accomplish this exposure, however.

Systematic desensitization is a technique for reducing fear or over-sensitivity based upon gradual exposure to the stimulus. The first step in a systematic desensitization plan is to teach the student some sort of coping skill (e.g., deep relaxation through deep breathing or muscle tensing/relaxing or perhaps physical contact). Following the development of this skill, one would then construct a hierarchy of phobic or uncomfortable stimuli, going from least anxiety-provoking or over-sensitive to most. If the issue was noise, for example, we might see what sounds or volumes were likely to cause disturbance and rank them according to aversiveness. The student would be helped to use his/her coping skills to achieve a state of relaxation. Following this, the stimuli from the hierarchy would be introduced, beginning with the least anxiety-provoking or least likely to cause overstimulation. In contrast to flooding, which we'll talk about next, we are trying to minimize any anxiety or discomfort. When any signs of discomfort were shown, the stimulus would be removed and the relaxation/coping restored. Only after calm had been re-established would the stimulus be reintroduced. When the student could experience that stimulus without discomfort, reinforcement would be provided and the next item would be introduced. This process would be repeated until the student could experience all items from the hierarchy without anxiety or overstimulation.

116

Flooding, in contrast, exposes the student to that which makes him/her anxious or overstimulated, in abundance. If a student is troubled by noises, (s)he might be brought into a noise-filled environment and allowed to desensitize all at once. The emphasis here is not on maintaining the relaxed/calm state, although of course that is preferable. The goal here is to simply have the student experience the unpleasant stimuli until fear or discomfort reactions are completely decreased. Obviously, this can be quite uncomfortable and many students are not able to provide the informed consent that would be necessary prior to providing such a procedure. Systematic desensitization is therefore preferable except in case of extreme mitigating circumstances.

104. Should we allow perseverative (self-stimulatory) behavior?

There are definitely two schools of thought on this matter. There are those who feel that "practice makes permanent" and that we should seek to eliminate the behavior entirely, lest continued practice make the behavior more and more a part of the individual's behavioral repertoire. Providing an alternate view are those who believe that the perseverative behavior should be allowed under controlled circumstances. Let's take these in turn.

Those who feel that "practice makes permanent" suggest that we must assume that the perseverative behavior is somehow being reinforced. The fact that it continues would support this notion. Behavior that is not reinforced does not simply continue without abating. In other words, by allowing the behavior to continue, we are allowing it to be reinforced and, by definition, become more probable and difficult to eventually extinguish.

Dissenting voices suggest that it would be impossible to truly prevent the behavior from *ever* occurring. When the individual is alone, (s)he can engage in the behavior. Some perseverative behavior is also extremely difficult to detect. We have all worked with students who perseverated on numbers and letters. How could you eliminate access to the stimuli? There are street signs, clocks, timers and visual cues of various sorts, they're everywhere!

As it will be impossible to eliminate the behavior entirely in some cases, so the reasoning goes, at least bring it under stimulus control. The student can engage in the perseverative behavior, but only in specified places and at specified times. In fact, we can allow the student to earn access to the behavior (through a token economy, for example). An adult consumer working in an outdoor area, for example, would abstain from perseverative rocking movements until he had earned a break period. During the break, he would go into a secluded room and be allowed to rock for a specified amount of time.

Let's refer back one last time to our answer from Chapter 1, Question #7: "it depends." Student variables and the behavior in question will likely determine which strategy you pursue.

105. Should we use aversives (punishers)?

This is probably the most emotionally-charged subject that one has to address within ABA programming (e.g., Sidman, 1989). By and large, behavior analysts come down very strongly against the use of aversives. Is this excessively idealistic, however? After all, don't parents of typically developing kids sometimes spank them? To understand why this is such a crucial area, and why behavior analysts generally advocate against the use of aversives, we need to analyze this issue in some detail. The text that follows was adapted from *Behaviorspeak* (Newman, Reeve, Reeve & Ryan, 2003).

An aversive is any consequence that serves as a positive punisher when immediately presented following a behavior (decreases the future probability of the preceding behavior), or whose removal serves as a negative reinforcer when removed following a behavior (increases the future probability of the preceding behavior).

A crucial fact that we need to appreciate is that aversives are every bit as individual as are reinforcers. What serves as a reinforcer for one student may serve as an aversive for another. To cite a domestic issue in the Reinecke-Newman house, there is absolutely no question what TIVO ™ has taped for Bobby, for Dana, or for our son David.

Behavior analysts generally avoid the use of aversives, as they may lead to many behavioral "side-effects."

    A.   The student may begin to avoid contact with the person delivering the aversive consequence.

    B.   The student may try to deliver an aversive towards the interventionist ("counter-aggression").

    C.   There will almost certainly be negative emotional responses.

D. The staff member may cease to function as a reinforcer.

E. The use of punishment is being modeled for a student we are teaching to imitate.

What makes this tricky is that aversives can be quite effective (at least temporarily) and therefore quite tempting to use. For example, if a staff member delivers an aversive to a student engaging in a dangerous behavior like darting into traffic, this contingent aversive will likely reduce the dangerous behavior. The act of delivering the aversive by the staff member has thus been negatively reinforced. As a result, the staff member may therefore be more likely to use an aversive in the future for less severe behavior (what we called in *Behaviorspeak* "using the death penalty for murder AND jay-walking").

There are two ethical principles to consider here. The Least Restrictive Treatment model, an ethical principle subscribed to by the vast majority of behavior analysts, tells us that we should not consider the use of aversives until we have *experimentally demonstrated with a stack of data up to your eyeballs that all less aversive treatments have been ineffective.* On the other hand, there is the Right to Effective Treatment. A student has the right to expect that you will use the most efficient means of teaching him/her skills and reducing inappropriate behavior. Is it ethically correct to allow me to bang my head while you try out less intrusive, but possibly less effective, techniques? The issue is murkier than many paint it to be, but we should all be able to agree that aversives should only be used in extreme circumstances when the behavioral stakes are quite high.

106. Should we use procedures like time out and response cost?

Time out and response cost are among the behavior reduction procedures. While powerful, they provide a very nice example of how and why we cannot simply create behavior management procedures without first conducting a functional analysis and considering individual learner characteristics.

Let's begin with *time out from positive reinforcement* (often called "time out" for short). This is perhaps the most misused of the behavior management techniques. The general method common to all true time out procedures is that a given reinforcer is removed for a short period of time, contingent upon the student displaying some behavior that has been targeted for reduction. While most people believe that this means having the student go to a different setting (e.g., the dreaded "time out" chair), time out does not need to take this form. We would argue that there are good reasons to avoid this form of time out. The individual needs to be supervised while in the time out setting, and this can accidentally reinforce the behavior you have targeted for reduction. Suppose that the behavior was actually serving an avoidance function. The time out, in effect, gives the student exactly what (s)he is looking for. The behavior targeted for reduction becomes the easiest way to avoid the undesired task. Inappropriate behavior often sky-rockets, and everyone wonders why.

For this reason, time out may more effectively take a more "inclusionary" form. A ribbon or badge being worn by a student, a symbol that indicates eligibility to receive other reinforcers, may be removed contingent upon inappropriate behavior (e.g., Foxx & Shapiro, 1978). A television may be temporarily turned off, contingent upon jumping or hand-flapping while watching. Either of these would be examples of inclusionary time-out. Either form of time-out can be effective, but the procedures must be designed carefully. If it is not truly a reinforcer that is being temporarily eliminated, or if the behavior is serving an avoidance function, the procedures can backfire.

Similarly, let's look at response cost. A response cost procedure is a form of negative punishment. When conducting response cost, a previously earned reinforcer is lost, contingent upon the displaying of a behavior targeted for reduction. A student working towards a given privilege on a token economy, for example, might lose a token if the targeted behavior was displayed.

Again, this procedure can be quite effective. There is also the potential for back-firing, however. If a student is able to lose tokens that have been earned, for example, there is a risk that the tokens may lose reinforcing value. Why work to earn something that might easily be taken away? Again, a careful consideration of the contingencies in place, and the student's reaction to them, is crucial. See Conyers et al. (2004) for a really nice empirical demonstration of just such considerations as regards response cost and differential reinforcement of other behavior.

Chapter XVII

Moving Towards Independence

107. How do we teach self-management?

Teaching self-management to students is one of the most effective ways to ensure continued programmatic success and maintenance of learned skills. Let's make the process a bit more concrete.

Self-management refers to a person performing two parallel procedures:

    A.   Self-monitoring

    B.   Self-reinforcement

People self-manage when they note their own behavior (self-monitoring) and deliver their own reinforcers (self-reinforcement), based upon satisfying the requirements of the target behavior (e.g., completing an academic assignment, or refraining from engaging in some specified behavior).

The teaching of self-management is generally a fading process. In the first phase, we begin with a standard teaching situation, indistinguishable from the Discrete Trial arrangement noted above. The interventionist prompts the behavior, assesses satisfaction of response criterion, and delivers consequences accordingly. We might call this "external reinforcement." Let's use as an example a student remaining on-task during academic instruction. At the end of each specified interval, the interventionist might deliver a token reinforcer if the student had been on-task the entire time.

Once the student has met criteria for performing the skill, we will begin fading towards self-management. To do so, we will begin the second phase, what we might call "prompted self-management" (we know it sounds like an oxymoron, but hang with us). When beginning a prompted self-management procedure, we fade back on the delivery of consequences, and fade towards a prompting stance (e.g., asking the student if (s)he has met criteria). For example, the student working in the academic context might be *asked* if he was on task (self-monitoring) and then prompted to take a token if he was. At first, the prompt would take the form of a direction to take the token if he was on-task. That prompt would then be faded to a question (e.g., "you did it right, you were paying attention the whole time, what should you do?"). As the student begins to successfully self-monitor and self-reinforce, fade back prompts still more. Instead of asking a question, allow the student to perform the self-monitoring and self-reinforcement tasks and then deliver consequences accordingly (e.g., reinforcing the act of appropriate self-reinforcement). When you reach this level, we naturally begin phase three.

The third phase is "unprompted self-management." In this phase of programming, all prompts to self-monitor and self-reinforce are withdrawn. It is a good idea to keep checks in place, however. Intermittent checks of student accuracy in self-management, and reinforcement for appropriate self-monitoring and self-reinforcement are a good idea. To complete our example, the student might be given a device that buzzes in his pocket at intervals. If the student had been on-task since the last buzz, he would give himself a token, and if not, he would not take the token. An outside staff member might also assess the student's on-task behavior and reinforce accuracy in token-taking.

As a final note on the matter, we generally try to fade token procedures or other more overt systems to become more and more inconspicuous as we work in mainstreaming settings. Token boards give way to check sheets in the student's own notebook, for example.

108. How do we teach initiations?

Teaching initiations is another place where many programs fall down. Too much (if not all) teaching takes the form of "teacher does this, then student does something, and then teacher delivers consequence based on student performance." This is, of course, the standard discrete trial teaching formula, isn't it? The problem however, is that old failure to generalize, combined with the dead man's test. I can't expect the student to spontaneously perform the same skill as an initiation as (s)he does in response to a teacher cue (see Newman & Ten Eyck, in press).

We generally want students to make socially-appropriate initiations that don't require prompting from another person. For example, we might want a student to walk into a room and say hello to whoever is in there, *without that other person having to say hello first.* Students who only say "hello" when spoken to first might appear unfriendly or strange. We want the behavior to occur in the presence of familiar people – not just in the presence of someone else saying "hello." That is, we want them to make the initiation spontaneously – not in response to someone else's greeting. (Note: we may also want to teach a student to respond to greetings spontaneously – saying "hello" in response to someone else's greeting – without prompting. Initiating greetings with familiar people and responding to greetings spontaneously are both important skills that may need to be taught separately.)

In order to teach initiations, paradoxically, one often begins by prompting them. This is most easily accomplished when there are two interventionists present. It is easier to have a second adult sitting behind a child, whispering in his/her ear to go over and make a statement to the first adult, than it is to have one adult whispering to the child "now you tell me." The first scenario lends itself to much easier fading, gradually reducing the input of the second adult as the student begins to perform the skill independently.

Another very useful method of prompting initiations is through scripting and script fading (e.g., Krantz & McClannahan, 1998). For students who can read, a textual representation of what you want them to say can be presented and then faded out. For non-readers, a voice recording or pictorial representation of the desired words and phrases can work just as well. Whatever prompting procedure is used, however, it is important that it is a true prompt and not an eliciting question or statement. For example, if we are teaching a student to initiate to others by introducing himself ("My name is John") the prompt would be either a verbal or written version of that statement. Saying "What is your name?" is **not** a prompt for an initiation; it is a question that will elicit a response. It is also extremely important to fade these prompts quickly.

Written prompts can be faded word-by-word; verbal prompts can also be faded by word or even by volume.

Chapter XVIII
Final Considerations

109. What is the "Clever Hans" effect?

Clever Hans was a horse that people mistakenly believed could perform mathematical operations. A math problem would be verbally posed to the horse, and seemingly miraculously, the horse could stomp his hoof the correct number of times to provide the solution to the problem.

The horse, of course, could not actually perform mathematical calculations (as far as we know). So what was happening here? It was discovered in the course of investigation that Hans was actually responding to subtle cues from his trainer (E.g., the horse would stomp his hoof as long as the trainer held his head down. The horse would stop stomping when the trainer looked up again).

In behavioral programming, we sometimes unwittingly create just such situations. The student learns not to attend to the stimuli in question, but to the interventionist. The interventionist who is not careful may provide cues in any number of subtle and unintended ways. Some of the most common include:

> A. Facial expressions that indicate approval or disapproval as the student reaches towards correct and incorrect choices.
>
> B. Putting correct stimuli in a particular position (on the right hand side more often than not, for example).

128

C.   Low level vocalizations.

D.   The interventionist tracking towards the correct choice with his/her eyes.

E.   The interventionist following a pattern of placing stimuli or otherwise setting up the teaching situation (see Lovaas, 2003 for some common "strategies" that students are often accidentally taught).

110. How can we ever thank you for putting this book together?

No problem, we were glad to do it.   If you are seeking reinforcers, however, Bobby's tastes run to 8-15 year old Bourbon and cigars from Honduras and Nicaragua. He also collects leather-bound copies of classic literature from Easton Press, as well as Zippo lighters.   Dana likes power tools and mystery novels. Tammy just wants peace on Earth and presents for her husband, Paul.

References and Suggested Reading

Arntzen, E. & Almas, I. K. (2002). Effects of mand-tact versus tact-only training on the acquisition of tacts. *Journal of Applied Behavior Analysis, 35,* 419-422.

Baer, D., Wolf, M., & Risley, T. (1968). Some current dimensions of applied behavior analysis. *Journal of Applied Behavior Analysis, 1* (1), 91-97.

Bailey, D. B., Hatton, D. D., Mesibov, G., Ament, N., & Skinner, M. (2000). Early development, temperament, and functional impairment in autism and fragile X syndrome. *Journal of Autism and Developmental Disorders, 30*(1), 49-59.

Barr-Berotti, D., Schwartz, L., Whitaker, L., Allgier, M., Garypie, L., Lawrence, M., Smith, C., Smart, J., and Teitelbaum, M. (2004). The Effects of Augmentative Communication Training on Speech: A Literature Review. Presented at the annual convention of the New York State Association for Behavior Analysis, Saratoga Springs.

Barrera, R. D., & Sulzer-Azaroff, B. (1983). An alternating treatment comparison of oral and total communication training programs with echolalic autistic children. *Journal of Applied Behavior Analysis, 16,* 379-394.

Bourret, J., Vollmer, T. R., and Rapp, J. T. (2004). Evaluation of a vocal mand assessment and vocal mand training procedures. *Journal of Applied Behavior Analysis, 37, 129-144.*

Carr, E. G., & Durand, V. M. (1985). Reducing behavior problems through functional communication training. *Journal of Applied Behavior Analysis, 18,* 111-126.

Carr, J. E., & Sidener, T. M. (2002). On the relation between applied behavior analysis and positive behavioral support. *The Behavior Analyst, 25,* 245-253.

Charlop-Christy, M.H., Carpenter, M.L., LeBlanc, L.A., & Kellet, K. (2002). Using the Picture Exchange Communication System (PECS) with children with autism: Assessment of PECS acquisition, speech, social-communicative behavior, and problem behavior. *Journal of Applied Behavior Analysis, 35,* 213-231.

Charlop, M. H. and Greenberg, F. (August 1985). Using ritualistic and stereotypic responses as reinforcers for autistic children, presented at the Annual Convention of the American Psychological Association, Los Angeles, CA.

Chiesa, M. (2004). ABA is not a therapy for autism. Presented at the conference for Parents Educated as Autism Therapists, Belfast, Northern Ireland.

Conyers, C., Miltenberger, R., Maki, A., Barenz, R., Jurgens, M., Sailer, A., Haugen, M., & Kopp, B. (2004). A comparison of response cost and differential reinforcement of other behavior to reduce dispute behavior in a preschool classroom. *Journal of Applied Behavior Analysis, 37, 411-415.*

Cooper, J. O., Heron, T. E., & Heward, W. L. (1987). *Applied behavior analysis.* Toronto: Merrill Publishing.

Davis, C. A., Brady, M. P., Williams, R. E., & Hamilton, R. (1992). Effects of high-probability requests on the acquisition and generalization of responses to requests in young children with behavior disorders. *Journal of Applied Behavior Analysis, 25,* 905-916.

Foxx, R. M. (1982). *Decreasing behaviors of persons with severe retardation and autism.* Champaign, IL: Research Press.

Foxx, R. M. (1982). *Increasing behaviors of persons with severe retardation and autism.* Champaign, IL: Research Press.

Foxx, R. M., & Shapiro, S. T. (1978). The timeout ribbon: A nonexlusionary timeout procedure. *Journal of Applied Behavior Analysis, 11,* 125–136.

Freeman, S. K., & Dake, L. (1997). *Teach me language.* Langley, British Columbia: SKF Books.

Green, G. (1996). Evaluating claims about treatments for autism. In C. Maurice, G. Green, & S. C. Luce (Eds.) *Behavioral intervention for young children with autism* (pp. 15-28). Austin, TX: Pro-Ed.

Ingersoll, B. D. & Goldstein, S. (1993). *Attention deficit disorder and learning disabilities: Realities, myths and controversial treatments.* New York: Main Street.

Jackson, L. & Panyan, M. V. (2002). *Positive behavioral support in the classroom: Principles and practices.* Baltimore: Paul H. Brookes.

Klin, A., Jones, W., Schultz, R., Volkmar, F., & Cohen, D. (2002). Visual Fixation patterns during viewing of naturalistic social situations as predictors of social competence in individuals with autism. *Archives of General Psychiatry, 59*, 809-816.

Krantz, P. J., & McClannahan, L. E. (1998). Social interaction skills for children with autism: A script-fading procedure for beginning readers. *Journal of Applied Behavior Analysis, 31*, 191-202.

Kravits, T. R., Kamps, D. M., Kemmerer, K., & Potucek, J. (2002). Brief Report: Increasing communication skills for an elementary-aged student with autism using the Picture Exchange Communication System. *Journal of Autism and Developmental Disorders, 32*, 225-230.

Lazarus, A. A. (1981). *The practice of multimodal therapy.* Baltimore: John Hopkins University Press.

Leaf, R. & McEachin, J. (1999). *A work in progress: Behavior management strategies and a curriculum for intensive behavioral treatment of autism.* New York: DRL Books, L.L.C.

Lovaas, O.I. (2003). *Teaching individuals with developmental delays: Basic intervention techniques.* Austin, TX: Pro-Ed.

Lovaas, O. I. (1987). Behavioral treatment and normal educational and intellectual functioning in young autistic children. *Journal of Consulting and Clinical Psychology, 55*, 3-9.

Lovaas, O. I. (1981). *Teaching developmentally disabled children: The ME book.* Austin, TX: Pro-Ed.

Maurice, C. (1993). *Let me hear your voice.* New York: Knopf.

Maurice, C., Green, G., & Luce, S. C. (1996). *Behavioral intervention for young children with autism.* Austin: Pro-Ed.

Needelman, M. (2000). My role as a related service provider at an ABA school for children with autism. In B. Newman, D. R. Reinecke, & L. Newman (Eds.), *Words from those who care: Further case studies of ABA with people with autism* (pp. 130-138). New York: Dove and Orca.

New York State Department of Health Early Intervention Program (1999). *Clinical practice guideline: Report of the recommendations, autism and pervasive developmental disorders.*

Newman, B. (2004). Elimination of aggression via a reversal of a sensory experience contingency. Presented at the annual conference of the New York State Association for Behavior Analysis.

Newman, B. (1999). *When everybody cares: Case studies of ABA with people with autism.* New York: Dove and Orca.

Newman, B. (1992). *The reluctant alliance: Behaviorism and humanism.* Buffalo, NY: Prometheus Books.

Newman, B., Needleman, M., Reinecke, D., & Robek, A. (2002). The effect of providing choices on skill acquisition and competing behavior of children with autism during discrete trial instruction. *Behavioral Intervention, 17,* 31-41.

Newman, B., Reeve, K. F., Reeve, S. A., & Ryan, C. S. (2003). *Behaviorspeak: A glossary of terms in applied behavior analysis.* New York: Dove and Orca.

134

Newman, B., Reinecke, D. R., Birch, S., & Blausten, F. G. (2002). *Graduated applied behavior analysis.* New York: Dove and Orca.

Newman, B., Reinecke, D. R., & Newman, L. (2000). *Words from those who care: Further case studies of ABA with people with autism.* New York: Dove and Orca.

Newman, B., & Ten Eyck, P. L. (in press). Self-management of social initiations by three children diagnosed with autism. *Analysis of Verbal Behavior.*

Odom, S. L., & Strain, P. S. (1986). A comparison of peer-initiation and teacher-antecedent interventions for promoting reciprocal social interaction of autistic preschoolers. *Journal of Applied Behavior Analysis, 19,* 59-71.

Page, T. J., Iwata, B. A., & Reid, D. H. (1982). Pyramidal training: A large-scale application with institutional staff. *Journal of Applied Behavior Analysis, 15,* 333-351.

Partington, J. (2004). Teaching skills to children with autism: Remembering to include the "analysis" in Applied Behavior Analysis programs. Presented at the annual conference of the New York State Association for Behavior Analysis, Saratoga Springs.

Romanczyk, R. G., Lockshin, S., & Matey, L. (1982/1996). *Individualized goal selection curriculum.* Apalachin, NY: Clinical Behavior Therapy Associates.

Schwartz, I. S., Garfinkle, A. N., & Bauer, J. (1998). The picture exchange communication system: Communicative outcomes for young children with disabilities. *Topics in Early Childhood Education, 18,* 144-159.

Sidman, M. (1989). *Coercion and its fallout.* Boston: Authors Cooperative.

Skinner, B. F. (1976). The ethics of helping people. *The Humanist, 36*(1), 7-11.

Skinner, B. F. (1974). *About behaviorism.* New York: Random House.

Skinner, B. F. (1972). Humanism and behaviorism. *The Humanist, 32*(4), 18-20.

Skinner, B. F. (1971). Humanistic behaviorism. *The Humanist, 31*(3), 35.

Skinner, B. F. (1957). *Verbal Behavior.* New York: Appleton-Ccentury Crofts.

Skinner, B. F. (1953). *Science and human behavior.* New York: The Free Press.

Stokes, T. F., & Baer, D. M. (1977). An implicit technology of generalization. *Journal of Applied Behavior Analysis, 10,* 349-367.

Stokes, T.F., & Osnes, P.G. (1988). The developing applied technology of generalization and maintenance. In R. Horner, G. Dunlap, & R.L. Koegel (Eds.), *Generalization and maintenance: Life-style changes in applied settings* (pp. 5-20). Baltimore: Brookes.

Sundberg, M. L., (2004). What would your day be like if you couldn't mand? Presented at the New York State Association for Behavior Analysis conference, White Plains, NY.

Sundberg, M. L., & Partington, J. W. (1998). *Teaching language to children with autism or other developmental disabilities.* Pleasant Hill, CA: Behavior Analysts.

Van Houten, R., Axelrod, S., Bailey, J. S., Favell, J. E., Foxx, R. M., Iwata, B. A., & Lovaas, O. I. (1988). The right to effective behavioral treatment. *Journal of Applied Behavior Analysis, 21*, 381-384.

About the Authors

Sir Robert Newman is a Board Certified Behavior Analyst and licensed psychologist. Affectionately known as the Dark Overlord of ABA, his past books include *When Everybody Cares, Words From Those who Care, Graduated Applied Behavior Analysis, No Virtue in Accident, The Reluctant Alliance,* and the wildly popular *Behaviorspeak* (with Ken Reeve, Sharon Reeve, and Carolyn Ryan). Bobby is the current President of the Association for Science in Autism Treatment and is a Past-President of the New York State Association for Behavior Analysis. He has consulted and designed programs for individuals of all ages diagnosed with autistic-spectrum disorders, throughout the United States, Canada, Ireland, England, and Northern Ireland. He works regularly with the programs of AMAC, Effective Interventions, and The Red Door. He has hosted a regular radio call-in program with the parents of the ELIJA Foundation. Dr. Newman has been honored for his work with individuals diagnosed with autistic-spectrum disorders by several parents' groups, and was knighted for his efforts by the F.A.I.T.H. (Focusing on Autism in the Home) parent's organization of Great Britain. Bobby is generally acknowledged as the sexiest male behavior analyst of all time. When they produce the film version of his life, he is not to be played by Woody Harrelson.

Tammy Hammond is a Board Certified Behavior Analyst. Tammy received a Bachelor of Arts from Transylvania University in Lexington, Kentucky, and a Master of Arts in Psychology at Binghamton University. She is completing her doctoral requirements in clinical psychology through Binghamton University. Tammy provides behavioral consultation for teachers and staff in special education and inclusion classrooms. She also provides training in ABA strategies at parent and teacher workshops and presents research at state and national conferences. Her two favorite pastimes are spending time with her family at "home" in Kentucky and working on remodeling projects with her husband, Paul, who cleverly entitled this book *Behaviorask.*

Dana Reinecke holds her doctorate in Psychology from the Learning Processes program of the Graduate School and University Center of the City University of New York. She consults with school programs for children with autism and is the Dean of Students for the American College of Applied Science. She is the author of several book chapters and articles on the behavioral treatment of autistic spectrum disorders, and has presented on these topics internationally. Dana is the loving and patient partner of Sir Robert, the world's sexiest behavior analyst, and the loving and patient mother of David, the overlordling.